THE COMPLETE CONFUCIUS

THE ANALECTS
THE DOCTRINE OF THE MEAN
THE GREAT LEARNING

With an introduction by Nicholas Tamblyn

GOLDING BOOKS

THE ESSENTIAL SERIES *by Golding Books*

The Complete Confucius
The Analects, The Doctrine of the
Mean, and The Great Learning

The Essential Tales of Horror
Frankenstein, The Fall of the
House of Usher, Strange Case of
Dr Jekyll and Mr Hyde, The Picture
of Dorian Gray, and Dracula

The Essential Classic Romances
Pride and Prejudice, Jane Eyre,
Wuthering Heights, and The Age
of Innocence

The Essential Louisa May Alcott
Little Women,
Little Men, and
Jo's Boys

Shakespeare's Sonnets

The Essential L. M. Montgomery
Anne of Green Gables, Anne of
Avonlea, Anne of the Island, and
Anne's House of Dreams

Jean-Christophe Complete

The Essential Robert Louis Stevenson
Treasure Island, Strange Case of
Dr Jekyll and My Hyde, Kidnapped,
and The Master of Ballantrae

The Essential Classics for Leaders
Tao Te Ching, The Art of War,
Meditations, and The Prince

The Essential Tales of Wonder
Alice's Adventures in Wonderland,
Through the Looking-Glass,
The Wonderful Wizard of Oz,
and Peter Pan

The Essential Willa Cather
O Pioneers!, The Song of the
Lark, My Ántonia, and
One of Ours

The Essential Mark Twain
The Adventures of Tom Sawyer,
Adventures of Huckleberry Finn,
The Prince and the Pauper, and
A Connecticut Yankee in
King Arthur's Court

The Essential Jules Verne
Journey to the Center of the Earth,
From the Earth to the Moon,
Twenty Thousand Leagues Under
The Sea, and Around the World
in Eighty Days

& Frances Hodgson Burnett
The Secret Garden, Little Lord
Fauntleroy, A Little Princess,
and The Lost Prince

Copyright © 2016, Nicholas Tamblyn. With translations by James Legge.

ISBN: 9781519096937

Cover design by SageStreetStudio.com. For the latest posts and
information about the author, visit NicholasTamblyn.com
as well as follow his updates on social media.

CONTENTS

INTRODUCTION

The man of virtue makes the difficulty to be overcome his first business, and success only a subsequent
consideration: this may be called perfect virtue.

—Chapter 6, *The Analects*

WE ARE BORN to a world—whether it be the traditional East or West, and everywhere in-between—that esteems Confucius as one of our very best thinkers, and a model for living a self-aware and virtuous life. Why is this?

First of all, for all of the diverse and unusual discussions, and occasional, thoughtful repetitions, he is eminently readable. His ideas make sense, and they are presented in a way that is ultimately (even in today's age of unlimited distractions) entertaining, and now and then they tend to the humorous.

Secondly, his ideas feel as modern and pertinent today as the day that his followers first inscribed them. He is a philosopher for every age, place, and time, concerned with integrity and a focus on true ethics. The unique group with which he holds his discourses probe issues relating to politics and leadership, friendship and love, and the complicated and ceaseless pursuits of success and sincerity.

Thirdly, it gives close intimations of who he was. Chapter 10 of *The Analects* describes many of his preferences and manners of living— referring to him as "simple and sincere"—and this book's preceding chapters, and the rest of his sayings and writings, show the spirit of someone who is deeply concerned with the day to day issues of one's customs and personal morals.

Finally, given each of these striking elements, over time Confucius has also remained compelling through his mystery. With all that there is in the texts, there are deep questions both at their heart and around the edges. His thoughts have come to be abundantly useful in all of our lives; and, beyond our speculation, this much can be said of the figure of Confucius, and the acute and instructive words that have been left to us.

NICHOLAS TAMBLYN

A NOTE ON THE ANALECTS

The Analects are a compilation of speeches by and conversations between Confucius and his disciples. Believed to have been written during China's Warring States period (475 BC–221 BC), and then finalized during the mid-Han dynasty (206 BC–220 AD), it is a collection of sayings and ideas that have a foremost position in the history and study of philosophy across the world.

Confucius lived from 551–479 BC. The principles he espoused largely reflected the values and traditions in China at the time. Rather than create a formal theory, Confucius desired that his disciples study, learning and mastering the classic older texts.

The Analects affirms that the superior person seeks and loves learning for the sake of learning, and righteousness for the sake of righteousness.

A NOTE ON THE DOCTRINE OF THE MEAN

From *The Book of Rites*, this chapter known as *The Doctrine of the Mean* is attributed to Confucius' only grandson, Zisi (also known as Kong Ji).

Its purpose is to show how the golden way is the means to gain perfect virtue, and that following the heavenly instructions of the Way will lead to the virtuous path trodden by others before, including Confucius.

The phrase "doctrine of the mean" ("zhōng yōng") first occurs in Chapter 6 of *The Analects*; its definition is not expanded on there, but Zisi's text seeks to examine its meaning in greater detail.

A NOTE ON THE GREAT LEARNING

Also one chapter in *The Book of Rites*, this writing is attributed to Confucius. In that book, his writing is accompanied by nine commentary chapters by his disciple Zeng Zi.

The Great Learning explores, in beautiful and scriptural-sounding language, the linked themes of self-cultivation, enquiry and examination, and their impacts upon leadership and government.

Each of the texts in this book—with *Mencius*, the collected conversations of that scholar with various kings—together comprise the four of the Four Books and Five Classics of Confucianism written in China before 300 BC.

THE ANALECTS

1

THE MASTER said, "Is it not pleasant to learn with a constant persever-
ance and application?

"Is it not delightful to have friends coming from distant quarters?

"Is he not a man of complete virtue, who feels no discomposure
though men may take no note of him?"

The philosopher Yu said, "They are few who, being filial and fraternal, are fond of offending against their superiors. There have been none,
who, not liking to offend against their superiors, have been fond of
stirring up confusion.

"The superior man bends his attention to what is radical. That being
established, all practical courses naturally grow up. Filial piety and fraternal submission!—are they not the root of all benevolent actions?"

The Master said, "Fine words and an insinuating appearance are seldom associated with true virtue."

The philosopher Tsang said, "I daily examine myself on three
points—whether, in transacting business for others, I may have been
not faithful; whether, in intercourse with friends, I may have been not
sincere; whether I may have not mastered and practiced the instructions of my teacher."

The Master said, "To rule a country of a thousand chariots, there
must be reverent attention to business, and sincerity; economy in expenditure, and love for men; and the employment of the people at the
proper seasons."

The Master said, "A youth, when at home, should be filial, and,
abroad, respectful to his elders. He should be earnest and truthful. He
should overflow in love to all, and cultivate the friendship of the good.
When he has time and opportunity, after the performance of these
things, he should employ them in polite studies."

Tsze-hsia said, "If a man withdraws his mind from the love of beauty, and applies it as sincerely to the love of the virtuous; if, in serving

his parents, he can exert his utmost strength; if, in serving his prince, he can devote his life; if, in his intercourse with his friends, his words are sincere—although men say that he has not learned, I will certainly say that he has."

The Master said, "If the scholar be not grave, he will not call forth any veneration, and his learning will not be solid.

"Hold faithfulness and sincerity as first principles.

"Have no friends not equal to yourself.

"When you have faults, do not fear to abandon them."

The philosopher Tsang said, "Let there be a careful attention to perform the funeral rites to parents, and let them be followed when long gone with the ceremonies of sacrifice—then the virtue of the people will resume its proper excellence."

Tsze-ch'in asked Tsze-kung saying, "When our master comes to any country, he does not fail to learn all about its government. Does he ask his information? or is it given to him?"

Tsze-kung said, "Our master is benign, upright, courteous, temperate, and complaisant and thus he gets his information. The master's mode of asking information—is it not different from that of other men?"

The Master said, "While a man's father is alive, look at the bent of his will; when his father is dead, look at his conduct. If for three years he does not alter from the way of his father, he may be called filial."

The philosopher Yu said, "In practicing the rules of propriety, a natural ease is to be prized. In the ways prescribed by the ancient kings, this is the excellent quality, and in things small and great we follow them.

"Yet it is not to be observed in all cases. If one, knowing how such ease should be prized, manifests it, without regulating it by the rules of propriety, this likewise is not to be done."

The philosopher Yu said, "When agreements are made according to what is right, what is spoken can be made good. When respect is shown according to what is proper, one keeps far from shame and disgrace. When the parties upon whom a man leans are proper persons to be intimate with, he can make them his guides and masters."

The Master said, "He who aims to be a man of complete virtue in his food does not seek to gratify his appetite, nor in his dwelling place does he seek the appliances of ease; he is earnest in what he is doing, and careful in his speech; he frequents the company of men of principle that he may be rectified—such a person may be said indeed to love to learn."

Tsze-kung said, "What do you pronounce concerning the poor man who yet does not flatter, and the rich man who is not proud?" The Master replied, "They will do; but they are not equal to him, who, though poor, is yet cheerful, and to him, who, though rich, loves the rules of propriety."

Tsze-kung replied, "It is said in the Book of Poetry, 'As you cut and then file, as you carve and then polish.'—The meaning is the same, I apprehend, as that which you have just expressed."

The Master said, "With one like Ts'ze, I can begin to talk about the odes. I told him one point, and he knew its proper sequence."

The Master said, "I will not be afflicted at men's not knowing me; I will be afflicted that I do not know men."

2

THE MASTER said, "He who exercises government by means of his virtue may be compared to the north polar star, which keeps its place and all the stars turn towards it."

The Master said, "In the Book of Poetry are three hundred pieces, but the design of them all may be embraced in one sentence, 'Having no depraved thoughts.'"

The Master said, "If the people be led by laws, and uniformity sought to be given them by punishments, they will try to avoid the punishment, but have no sense of shame.

"If they be led by virtue, and uniformity sought to be given them by the rules of propriety, they will have the sense of shame, and moreover will become good."

The Master said, "At fifteen, I had my mind bent on learning.

"At thirty, I stood firm.

"At forty, I had no doubts.

"At fifty, I knew the decrees of Heaven.

"At sixty, my ear was an obedient organ for the reception of truth.

"At seventy, I could follow what my heart desired, without transgressing what was right."

Mang I asked what filial piety was. The Master said, "It is not being disobedient."

Soon after, as Fan Ch'ih was driving him, the Master told him, saying, "Mang-sun asked me what filial piety was, and I answered him, 'not being disobedient.'"

Fan Ch'ih said, "What did you mean?" The Master replied, "That parents, when alive, be served according to propriety; that, when dead, they should be buried according to propriety; and that they should be sacrificed to according to propriety."

Mang Wu asked what filial piety was. The Master said, "Parents are anxious lest their children should be sick."

Tsze-yu asked what filial piety was. The Master said, "The filial piety nowadays means the support of one's parents. But dogs and horses likewise are able to do something in the way of support—without reverence, what is there to distinguish the one support given from the other?"

Tsze-hsia asked what filial piety was. The Master said, "The difficulty is with the countenance. If, when their elders have any troublesome affairs, the young take the toil of them, and if, when the young have wine and food, they set them before their elders, is THIS to be considered filial piety?"

The Master said, "I have talked with Hui for a whole day, and he has not made any objection to anything I said—as if he were stupid. He has retired, and I have examined his conduct when away from me, and found him able to illustrate my teachings. Hui!—He is not stupid."

The Master said, "See what a man does.

"Mark his motives.

"Examine in what things he rests.

"How can a man conceal his character? How can a man conceal his character?"

The Master said, "If a man keeps cherishing his old knowledge, so as continually to be acquiring new, he may be a teacher of others."

The Master said, "The accomplished scholar is not a utensil."

Tsze-kung asked what constituted the superior man. The Master said, "He acts before he speaks, and afterwards speaks according to his actions."

The Master said, "The superior man is catholic and not partisan. The mean man is partisan and not catholic."

The Master said, "Learning without thought is labor lost; thought without learning is perilous."

The Master said, "The study of strange doctrines is injurious indeed!"

The Master said, "Yu, shall I teach you what knowledge is? When you know a thing, to hold that you know it; and when you do not know a thing, to allow that you do not know it—this is knowledge."

Tsze-chang was learning with a view to official emolument.

The Master said, "Hear much and put aside the points of which you stand in doubt, while you speak cautiously at the same time of the others—then you will afford few occasions for blame. See much and put aside the things which seem perilous, while you are cautious at the same time in carrying the others into practice: then you will have few occasions for repentance. When one gives few occasions for blame in his words, and few occasions for repentance in his conduct, he is in the way to get emolument."

The Duke Ai asked, saying, "What should be done in order to secure the submission of the people?" Confucius replied, "Advance the upright and set aside the crooked, then the people will submit. Advance the crooked and set aside the upright, then the people will not submit."

Chi K'ang asked how to cause the people to reverence their ruler, to be faithful to him, and to go on to nerve themselves to virtue. The Master said, "Let him preside over them with gravity—then they will reverence him. Let him be final and kind to all—then they will be faithful to him. Let him advance the good and teach the incompetent—then they will eagerly seek to be virtuous."

Some one addressed Confucius, saying, "Sir, why are you not engaged in the government?"

The Master said, "What does the Shu-ching say of filial piety?—'You are final, you discharge your brotherly duties. These qualities are displayed in government.' This then also constitutes the exercise of government. Why must there be THAT—making one be in the government?"

The Master said, "I do not know how a man without truthfulness is to get on. How can a large carriage be made to go without the crossbar for yoking the oxen to, or a small carriage without the arrangement for yoking the horses?"

Tsze-chang asked whether the affairs of ten ages after could be known.

Confucius said, "The Yin dynasty followed the regulations of the Hsia: wherein it took from or added to them may be known. The Chau dynasty has followed the regulations of Yin: wherein it took from or added to them may be known. Some other may follow the Chau, but though it should be at the distance of a hundred ages, its affairs may be known."

The Master said, "For a man to sacrifice to a spirit which does not belong to him is flattery.

"To see what is right and not to do it is want of courage."

3

CONFUCIUS SAID of the head of the Chi family, who had eight rows of pantomimes in his area, "If he can bear to do this, what may he not bear to do?"

The three families used the Yungode, while the vessels were being removed, at the conclusion of the sacrifice. The Master said, "'Assisting are the princes—the son of heaven looks profound and grave'—what application can these words have in the hall of the three families?"

The Master said, "If a man be without the virtues proper to humanity, what has he to do with the rites of propriety? If a man be without the virtues proper to humanity, what has he to do with music?"

Lin Fang asked what was the first thing to be attended to in ceremonies.

The Master said, "A great question indeed!

"In festive ceremonies, it is better to be sparing than extravagant. In the ceremonies of mourning, it is better that there be deep sorrow than in minute attention to observances."

The Master said, "The rude tribes of the east and north have their princes, and are not like the States of our great land which are without them."

The chief of the Chi family was about to sacrifice to the T'ai mountain. The Master said to Zan Yu, "Can you not save him from this?" He answered, "I cannot." Confucius said, "Alas! will you say that the T'ai mountain is not so discerning as Lin Fang?"

The Master said, "The student of virtue has no contentions. If it be said he cannot avoid them, shall this be in archery? But he bows complaisantly to his competitors; thus he ascends the hall, descends, and exacts the forfeit of drinking. In his contention, he is still the Chun-tsze."

Tsze-hsia asked, saying, "What is the meaning of the passage—'The pretty dimples of her artful smile! The well-defined black and white of her eye! The plain ground for the colors?'"

The Master said, "The business of laying on the colors follows the preparation of the plain ground."

"Ceremonies then are a subsequent thing?" The Master said, "It is Shang who can bring out my meaning. Now I can begin to talk about the odes with him."

The Master said, "I could describe the ceremonies of the Hsia dynasty, but Chi cannot sufficiently attest my words. I could describe the ceremonies of the Yin dynasty, but Sung cannot sufficiently attest my words. They cannot do so because of the insufficiency of their records and wise men. If those were sufficient, I could adduce them in support of my words."

The Master said, "At the great sacrifice, after the pouring out of the libation, I have no wish to look on."

Some one asked the meaning of the great sacrifice. The Master said, "I do not know. He who knew its meaning would find it as easy to govern the kingdom as to look on this"—pointing to his palm.

He sacrificed to the dead, as if they were present. He sacrificed to the spirits, as if the spirits were present.

The Master said, "I consider my not being present at the sacrifice, as if I did not sacrifice."

Wang-sun Chia asked, saying, "What is the meaning of the saying, 'It is better to pay court to the furnace than to the southwest corner?'"

The Master said, "Not so. He who offends against Heaven has none to whom he can pray."

The Master said, "Chau had the advantage of viewing the two past dynasties. How complete and elegant are its regulations! I follow Chau."

The Master, when he entered the grand temple, asked about everything. Some one said, "Who say that the son of the man of Tsau knows the rules of propriety! He has entered the grand temple and asks about everything." The Master heard the remark, and said, "This is a rule of propriety."

The Master said, "In archery it is not going through the leather which is the principal thing—because people's strength is not equal. This was the old way."

Tsze-kung wished to do away with the offering of a sheep connected with the inauguration of the first day of each month.

The Master said, "Ts'ze, you love the sheep; I love the ceremony."

The Master said, "The full observance of the rules of propriety in serving one's prince is accounted by people to be flattery."

The Duke Ting asked how a prince should employ his ministers, and how ministers should serve their prince. Confucius replied, "A prince should employ his minister according to the rules of propriety; ministers should serve their prince with faithfulness."

The Master said, "The Kwan Tsu is expressive of enjoyment without being licentious, and of grief without being hurtfully excessive."

The Duke Ai asked Tsai Wo about the altars of the spirits of the land. Tsai Wo replied, "The Hsia sovereign planted the pine tree about them; the men of the Yin planted the cypress; and the men of the Chau planted the chestnut tree, meaning thereby to cause the people to be in awe."

When the Master heard it, he said, "Things that are done, it is needless to speak about; things that have had their course, it is needless to remonstrate about; things that are past, it is needless to blame."

The Master said, "Small indeed was the capacity of Kwan Chung!"

Some one said, "Was Kwan Chung parsimonious?" "Kwan," was the reply, "had the San Kwei, and his officers performed no double duties; how can he be considered parsimonious?"

"Then, did Kwan Chung know the rules of propriety?" The Master said, "The princes of States have a screen intercepting the view at their gates. Kwan had likewise a screen at his gate. The princes of States on any friendly meeting between two of them, had a stand on which to place their inverted cups. Kwan had also such a stand. If Kwan knew the rules of propriety, who does not know them?"

The Master instructing the grand music master of Lu said, "How to play music may be known. At the commencement of the piece, all the parts should sound together. As it proceeds, they should be in harmony while severally distinct and flowing without break, and thus on to the conclusion."

The border warden at Yi requested to be introduced to the Master, saying, "When men of superior virtue have come to this, I have never been denied the privilege of seeing them." The followers of the sage introduced him, and when he came out from the interview, he said, "My friends, why are you distressed by your master's loss of office?

The kingdom has long been without the principles of truth and right; Heaven is going to use your master as a bell with its wooden tongue."

The Master said of the Shao that it was perfectly beautiful and also perfectly good. He said of the Wu that it was perfectly beautiful but not perfectly good.

The Master said, "High station filled without indulgent generosity; ceremonies performed without reverence; mourning conducted without sorrow—wherewith should I contemplate such ways?"

4

THE MASTER said, "It is virtuous manners which constitute the excellence of a neighborhood. If a man in selecting a residence do not fix on one where such prevail, how can he be wise?"

The Master said, "Those who are without virtue cannot abide long either in a condition of poverty and hardship, or in a condition of enjoyment. The virtuous rest in virtue; the wise desire virtue."

The Master said, "It is only the truly virtuous man, who can love, or who can hate, others."

The Master said, "If the will be set on virtue, there will be no practice of wickedness."

The Master said, "Riches and honors are what men desire. If they cannot be obtained in the proper way, they should not be held. Poverty and meanness are what men dislike. If they cannot be avoided in the proper way, they should not be avoided.

"If a superior man abandon virtue, how can he fulfill the requirements of that name?

"The superior man does not, even for the space of a single meal, act contrary to virtue. In moments of haste, he cleaves to it. In seasons of danger, he cleaves to it."

The Master said, "I have not seen a person who loved virtue, or one who hated what was not virtuous. He who loved virtue, would esteem nothing above it. He who hated what is not virtuous, would practice virtue in such a way that he would not allow anything that is not virtuous to approach his person.

"Is any one able for one day to apply his strength to virtue? I have not seen the case in which his strength would be insufficient.

"Should there possibly be any such case, I have not seen it."

The Master said, "The faults of men are characteristic of the class to which they belong. By observing a man's faults, it may be known that he is virtuous."

The Master said, "If a man in the morning hear the right way, he may die in the evening hear regret."

The Master said, "A scholar, whose mind is set on truth, and who is ashamed of bad clothes and bad food, is not fit to be discoursed with."

The Master said, "The superior man, in the world, does not set his mind either for anything, or against anything; what is right he will follow."

The Master said, "The superior man thinks of virtue; the small man thinks of comfort. The superior man thinks of the sanctions of law; the small man thinks of favors which he may receive."

The Master said: "He who acts with a constant view to his own advantage will be much murmured against."

The Master said, "If a prince is able to govern his kingdom with the complaisance proper to the rules of propriety, what difficulty will he have? If he cannot govern it with that complaisance, what has he to do with the rules of propriety?"

The Master said, "A man should say, I am not concerned that I have no place, I am concerned how I may fit myself for one. I am not concerned that I am not known, I seek to be worthy to be known."

The Master said, "Shan, my doctrine is that of an all-pervading unity." The disciple Tsang replied, "Yes."

The Master went out, and the other disciples asked, saying, "What do his words mean?" Tsang said, "The doctrine of our master is to be true to the principles—of our nature and the benevolent exercise of them to others—this and nothing more."

The Master said, "The mind of the superior man is conversant with righteousness; the mind of the mean man is conversant with gain."

The Master said, "When we see men of worth, we should think of equaling them; when we see men of a contrary character, we should turn inwards and examine ourselves."

The Master said, "In serving his parents, a son may remonstrate with them, but gently; when he sees that they do not incline to follow his advice, he shows an increased degree of reverence, but does not abandon his purpose; and should they punish him, he does not allow himself to murmur."

The Master said, "While his parents are alive, the son may not go abroad to a distance. If he does go abroad, he must have a fixed place to which he goes."

The Master said, "If the son for three years does not alter from the way of his father, he may be called filial."

The Master said, "The years of parents may by no means not be kept in the memory, as an occasion at once for joy and for fear."

The Master said, "The reason why the ancients did not readily give utterance to their words, was that they feared lest their actions should not come up to them."

The Master said, "The cautious seldom err."

The Master said, "The superior man wishes to be slow in his speech and earnest in his conduct."

The Master said, "Virtue is not left to stand alone. He who practices it will have neighbors."

Tsze-yu said, "In serving a prince, frequent remonstrances lead to disgrace. Between friends, frequent reproofs make the friendship distant."

5

THE MASTER said of Kung-ye Ch'ang that he might be wived; although he was put in bonds, he had not been guilty of any crime. Accordingly, he gave him his own daughter to wife.

Of Nan Yung he said that if the country were well governed he would not be out of office, and if it were in governed, he would escape punishment and disgrace. He gave him the daughter of his own elder brother to wife.

The Master said of Tsze-chien, "Of superior virtue indeed is such a man! If there were not virtuous men in Lu, how could this man have acquired this character?"

Tsze-kung asked, "What do you say of me, Ts'ze!" The Master said, "You are a utensil." "What utensil?" "A gemmed sacrificial utensil."

Some one said, "Yung is truly virtuous, but he is not ready with his tongue."

The Master said, "What is the good of being ready with the tongue? They who encounter men with smartness of speech for the most part procure themselves hatred. I know not whether he be truly virtuous, but why should he show readiness of the tongue?"

The Master was wishing Ch'i-tiao K'ai to enter an official employment. He replied, "I am not yet able to rest in the assurance of this." The Master was pleased.

The Master said, "My doctrines make no way. I will get upon a raft, and float about on the sea. He that will accompany me will be Yu, I dare say." Tsze-lu hearing this was glad, upon which the Master said, "Yu is fonder of daring than I am. He does not exercise his judgment upon matters."

Mang Wu asked about Tsze-lu, whether he was perfectly virtuous. The Master said, "I do not know."

He asked again, when the Master replied, "In a kingdom of a thousand chariots, Yu might be employed to manage the military levies, but I do not know whether he be perfectly virtuous."

"And what do you say of Ch'iu?" The Master replied, "In a city of a thousand families, or a clan of a hundred chariots, Ch'iu might be employed as governor, but I do not know whether he is perfectly virtuous."

"What do you say of Ch'ih?" The Master replied, "With his sash girt and standing in a court, Ch'ih might be employed to converse with the visitors and guests, but I do not know whether he is perfectly virtuous."

The Master said to Tsze-kung, "Which do you consider superior, yourself or Hui?"

Tsze-kung replied, "How dare I compare myself with Hui? Hui hears one point and knows all about a subject; I hear one point, and know a second."

The Master said, "You are not equal to him. I grant you, you are not equal to him."

Tsai Yu being asleep during the daytime, the Master said, "Rotten wood cannot be carved; a wall of dirty earth will not receive the trowel. This Yu—what is the use of my reproving him?"

The Master said, "At first, my way with men was to hear their words, and give them credit for their conduct. Now my way is to hear their words, and look at their conduct. It is from Yu that I have learned to make this change."

The Master said, "I have not seen a firm and unbending man." Some one replied, "There is Shan Ch'ang." "Ch'ang," said the Master, "is under the influence of his passions; how can he be pronounced firm and unbending?"

Tsze-kung said, "What I do not wish men to do to me, I also wish not to do to men." The Master said, "Ts'ze, you have not attained to that."

Tsze-kung said, "The Master's personal displays of his principles and ordinary descriptions of them may be heard. His discourses about man's nature, and the way of Heaven, cannot be heard."

When Tsze-lu heard anything, if he had not yet succeeded in carrying it into practice, he was only afraid lest he should hear something else.

Tsze-kung asked, saying, "On what ground did Kung-wan get that title of Wan?"

The Master said, "He was of an active nature and yet fond of learning, and he was not ashamed to ask and learn of his inferiors!—On these grounds he has been styled Wan."

The Master said of Tsze-ch'an that he had four of the characteristics of a superior man—in his conduct of himself, he was humble; in serving his superior, he was respectful; in nourishing the people, he was kind; in ordering the people, he was just."

The Master said, "Yen P'ing knew well how to maintain friendly intercourse. The acquaintance might be long, but he showed the same respect as at first."

The Master said, "Tsang Wan kept a large tortoise in a house, on the capitals of the pillars of which he had hills made, and with representations of duckweed on the small pillars above the beams supporting the rafters.—Of what sort was his wisdom?"

Tsze-chang asked, saying, "The minister Tsze-wan thrice took office, and manifested no joy in his countenance. Thrice he retired from office, and manifested no displeasure. He made it a point to inform the new minister of the way in which he had conducted the government; what do you say of him?" The Master replied. "He was loyal." "Was he perfectly virtuous?" "I do not know. How can he be pronounced perfectly virtuous?"

Tsze-chang proceeded, "When the officer Ch'ui killed the prince of Ch'i, Ch'an Wan, though he was the owner of forty horses, abandoned them and left the country. Coming to another state, he said, 'They are here like our great officer, Ch'ui,' and left it. He came to a second state, and with the same observation left it also—what do you say of him?" The Master replied, "He was pure." "Was he perfectly virtuous?" "I do not know. How can he be pronounced perfectly virtuous?"

Chi Wan thought thrice, and then acted. When the Master was informed of it, he said, "Twice may do."

The Master said, "When good order prevailed in his country, Ning Wu acted the part of a wise man. When his country was in disorder, he acted the part of a stupid man. Others may equal his wisdom, but they cannot equal his stupidity."

When the Master was in Ch'an, he said, "Let me return! Let me return! The little children of my school are ambitious and too hasty. They are accomplished and complete so far, but they do not know how to restrict and shape themselves."

The Master said, "Po-i and Shu-ch'i did not keep the former wickednesses of men in mind, and hence the resentments directed towards them were few."

The Master said, "Who says of Weishang Kao that he is upright? One begged some vinegar of him, and he begged it of a neighbor and gave it to the man."

The Master said, "Fine words, an insinuating appearance, and excessive respect—Tso Ch'iu-ming was ashamed of them. I also am ashamed of them. To conceal resentment against a person, and appear friendly with him—Tso Ch'iu-ming was ashamed of such conduct. I also am ashamed of it."

Yen Yuan and Chi Lu being by his side, the Master said to them, "Come, let each of you tell his wishes."

Tsze-lu said, "I should like, having chariots and horses, and light fur clothes, to share them with my friends, and though they should spoil them, I would not be displeased."

Yen Yuan said, "I should like not to boast of my excellence, nor to make a display of my meritorious deeds."

Tsze-lu then said, "I should like, sir, to hear your wishes." The Master said, "They are, in regard to the aged, to give them rest; in regard to friends, to show them sincerity; in regard to the young, to treat them tenderly."

The Master said, "It is all over. I have not yet seen one who could perceive his faults, and inwardly accuse himself."

The Master said, "In a hamlet of ten families, there may be found one honorable and sincere as I am, but not so fond of learning."

THE MASTER said, "There is Yung!—He might occupy the place of a prince."

Chung-kung asked about Tsze-sang Po-tsze. The Master said, "He may pass. He does not mind small matters."

Chung-kung said, "If a man cherish in himself a reverential feeling of the necessity of attention to business, though he may be easy in small matters in his government of the people, that may be allowed. But if he cherish in himself that easy feeling, and also carry it out in his practice, is not such an easy mode of procedure excessive?"

The Master said, "Yung's words are right."

The Duke Ai asked which of the disciples loved to learn.

Confucius replied to him, "There was Yen Hui; he loved to learn. He did not transfer his anger; he did not repeat a fault. Unfortunately, his appointed time was short and he died; and now there is not such another. I have not yet heard of any one who loves to learn as he did."

Tsze-hwa being employed on a mission to Ch'i, the disciple Zan requested grain for his mother. The Master said, "Give her a fu." Yen requested more. "Give her a yi," said the Master. Yen gave her five ping.

The Master said, "When Ch'ih was proceeding to Ch'i, he had fat horses to his carriage, and wore light furs. I have heard that a superior man helps the distressed, but does not add to the wealth of the rich."

Yuan Sze being made governor of his town by the Master, he gave him nine hundred measures of grain, but Sze declined them.

The Master said, "Do not decline them. May you not give them away in the neighborhoods, hamlets, towns, and villages?"

The Master, speaking of Chung-kung, said, "If the calf of a brindled cow be red and homed, although men may not wish to use it, would the spirits of the mountains and rivers put it aside?"

The Master said, "Such was Hui that for three months there would be nothing in his mind contrary to perfect virtue. The others may attain to this on some days or in some months, but nothing more."

Chi K'ang asked about Chung-yu, whether he was fit to be employed as an officer of government. The Master said, "Yu is a man of decision; what difficulty would he find in being an officer of government?" K'ang asked, "Is Ts'ze fit to be employed as an officer of government?" and was answered, "Ts'ze is a man of intelligence; what difficulty would he find in being an officer of government?" And to the same question about Ch'iu the Master gave the same reply, saying, "Ch'iu is a man of various ability."

The chief of the Chi family sent to ask Min Tsze-ch'ien to be governor of Pi. Min Tszech'ien said, "Decline the offer for me politely. If any one come again to me with a second invitation, I shall be obliged to go and live on the banks of the Wan."

Po-niu being ill, the Master went to ask for him. He took hold of his hand through the window, and said, "It is killing him. It is the appointment of Heaven, alas! That such a man should have such a sickness! That such a man should have such a sickness!"

The Master said, "Admirable indeed was the virtue of Hui! With a single bamboo dish of rice, a single gourd dish of drink, and living in his mean narrow lane, while others could not have endured the distress, he did not allow his joy to be affected by it. Admirable indeed was the virtue of Hui!"

Yen Ch'iu said, "It is not that I do not delight in your doctrines, but my strength is insufficient." The Master said, "Those whose strength is insufficient give over in the middle of the way but now you limit yourself."

The Master said to Tsze-hsia, "Do you be a scholar after the style of the superior man, and not after that of the mean man."

Tsze-yu being governor of Wu-ch'ang, the Master said to him, "Have you got good men there?" He answered, "There is Tan-t'ai Miehming, who never in walking takes a short cut, and never comes to my office, excepting on public business."

The Master said, "Mang Chih-fan does not boast of his merit. Being in the rear on an occasion of flight, when they were about to enter the gate, he whipped up his horse, saying, 'It is not that I dare to be last. My horse would not advance.'"

The Master said, "Without the specious speech of the litanist T'o and the beauty of the prince Chao of Sung, it is difficult to escape in the present age."

The Master said, "Who can go out but by the door? How is it that men will not walk according to these ways?"

The Master said, "Where the solid qualities are in excess of accomplishments, we have rusticity; where the accomplishments are in excess of the solid qualities, we have the manners of a clerk. When the accomplishments and solid qualities are equally blended, we then have the man of virtue."

The Master said, "Man is born for uprightness. If a man lose his uprightness, and yet live, his escape from death is the effect of mere good fortune."

The Master said, "They who know the truth are not equal to those who love it, and they who love it are not equal to those who delight in it."

The Master said, "To those whose talents are above mediocrity, the highest subjects may be announced. To those who are below mediocrity, the highest subjects may not be announced."

Fan Ch'ih asked what constituted wisdom. The Master said, "To give one's self earnestly to the duties due to men, and, while respecting spiritual beings, to keep aloof from them, may be called wisdom." He asked about perfect virtue. The Master said, "The man of virtue makes the difficulty to be overcome his first business, and success only a subsequent consideration: this may be called perfect virtue."

The Master said, "The wise find pleasure in water; the virtuous find pleasure in hills. The wise are active; the virtuous are tranquil. The wise are joyful; the virtuous are long-lived."

The Master said, "Ch'i, by one change, would come to the State of Lu. Lu, by one change, would come to a State where true principles predominated."

The Master said, "A cornered vessel without corners—a strange cornered vessel! A strange cornered vessel!"

Tsai Wo asked, saying, "A benevolent man, though it be told him—'There is a man in the well,' will go in after him, I suppose." Confucius said, "Why should he do so? A superior man may be made to go to the well, but he cannot be made to go down into it. He may be imposed upon, but he cannot be fooled."

The Master said, "The superior man, extensively studying all learning, and keeping himself under the restraint of the rules of propriety, may thus likewise not overstep what is right."

The Master having visited Nan-tsze, Tsze-lu was displeased, on which the Master swore, saying, "Wherein I have done improperly, may Heaven reject me, may Heaven reject me!"

The Master said, "Perfect is the virtue which is according to the Constant Mean! Rare for a long time has been its practice among the people."

Tsze-kung said, "Suppose the case of a man extensively conferring benefits on the people, and able to assist all, what would you say of him? Might he be called perfectly virtuous?" The Master said, "Why speak only of virtue in connection with him? Must he not have the qualities of a sage? Even Yao and Shun were still solicitous about this.

"Now the man of perfect virtue, wishing to be established himself, seeks also to establish others; wishing to be enlarged himself, he seeks also to enlarge others.

"To be able to judge of others by what is nigh in ourselves;—this may be called the art of virtue."

7

THE MASTER said, "A transmitter and not a maker, believing in and loving the ancients, I venture to compare myself with our old P'ang."

The Master said, "The silent treasuring up of knowledge; learning without satiety; and instructing others without being wearied—which one of these things belongs to me?"

The Master said, "The leaving virtue without proper cultivation; the not thoroughly discussing what is learned; not being able to move towards righteousness of which a knowledge is gained; and not being able to change what is not good—these are the things which occasion me solicitude."

When the Master was unoccupied with business, his manner was easy, and he looked pleased.

The Master said, "Extreme is my decay. For a long time, I have not dreamed, as I was wont to do, that I saw the duke of Chau."

The Master said, "Let the will be set on the path of duty.

"Let every attainment in what is good be firmly grasped.

"Let perfect virtue be accorded with.

"Let relaxation and enjoyment be found in the polite arts."

The Master said, "From the man bringing his bundle of dried flesh for my teaching upwards, I have never refused instruction to any one."

The Master said, "I do not open up the truth to one who is not eager to get knowledge, nor help out any one who is not anxious to explain himself. When I have presented one corner of a subject to any one, and he cannot from it learn the other three, I do not repeat my lesson."

When the Master was eating by the side of a mourner, he never ate to the full.

He did not sing on the same day in which he had been weeping.

The Master said to Yen Yuan, "When called to office, to undertake its duties; when not so called, to he retired—it is only I and you who have attained to this."

Tsze-lu said, "If you had the conduct of the armies of a great state, whom would you have to act with you?"

The Master said, "I would not have him to act with me, who will unarmed attack a tiger, or cross a river without a boat, dying without any regret. My associate must be the man who proceeds to action full of solicitude, who is fond of adjusting his plans, and then carries them into execution."

The Master said, "If the search for riches is sure to be successful, though I should become a groom with whip in hand to get them, I will do so. As the search may not be successful, I will follow after that which I love."

The things in reference to which the Master exercised the greatest caution were—fasting, war, and sickness.

When the Master was in Ch'i, he heard the Shao, and for three months did not know the taste of flesh. "I did not think," he said, "that music could have been made so excellent as this."

Yen Yu said, "Is our Master for the ruler of Wei?" Tsze-kung said, "Oh! I will ask him."

He went in accordingly, and said, "What sort of men were Po-i and Shu-ch'i?" "They were ancient worthies," said the Master. "Did they have any repinings because of their course?" The Master again replied, "They sought to act virtuously, and they did so; what was there for them to repine about?" On this, Tsze-kung went out and said, "Our Master is not for him."

The Master said, "With coarse rice to eat, with water to drink, and my bended arm for a pillow—I have still joy in the midst of these things. Riches and honors acquired by unrighteousness, are to me as a floating cloud."

The Master said, "If some years were added to my life, I would give fifty to the study of the Yi, and then I might come to be without great faults."

The Master's frequent themes of discourse were—the Odes, the History, and the maintenance of the Rules of Propriety. On all these he frequently discoursed.

The Duke of Sheh asked Tsze-lu about Confucius, and Tsze-lu did not answer him.

The Master said, "Why did you not say to him—He is simply a man, who in his eager pursuit of knowledge forgets his food, who in the joy of its attainment forgets his sorrows, and who does not perceive that old age is coming on?"

The Master said, "I am not one who was born in the possession of knowledge; I am one who is fond of antiquity, and earnest in seeking it there."

The subjects on which the Master did not talk, were—extraordinary things, feats of strength, disorder, and spiritual beings.

The Master said, "When I walk along with two others, they may serve me as my teachers. I will select their good qualities and follow them, their bad qualities and avoid them."

The Master said, "Heaven produced the virtue that is in me. Hwan T'ui—what can he do to me?"

The Master said, "Do you think, my disciples, that I have any concealments? I conceal nothing from you. There is nothing which I do that is not shown to you, my disciples; that is my way."

There were four things which the Master taught—letters, ethics, devotion of soul, and truthfulness.

The Master said, "A sage it is not mine to see; could I see a man of real talent and virtue, that would satisfy me."

The Master said, "A good man it is not mine to see; could I see a man possessed of constancy, that would satisfy me.

"Having not and yet affecting to have, empty and yet affecting to be full, straitened and yet affecting to be at ease—it is difficult with such characteristics to have constancy."

The Master angled—but did not use a net. He shot—but not at birds perching.

The Master said, "There may be those who act without knowing why. I do not do so. Hearing much and selecting what is good and following it; seeing much and keeping it in memory: this is the second style of knowledge."

It was difficult to talk profitably and reputably with the people of Hu-hsiang, and a lad of that place having had an interview with the Master, the disciples doubted.

The Master said, "I admit people's approach to me without committing myself as to what they may do when they have retired. Why must one be so severe? If a man purify himself to wait upon me, I receive him so purified, without guaranteeing his past conduct."

The Master said, "Is virtue a thing remote? I wish to be virtuous, and lo! virtue is at hand."

The minister of crime of Ch'an asked whether the duke Chao knew propriety, and Confucius said, "He knew propriety."

Confucius having retired, the minister bowed to Wu-ma Ch'i to come forward, and said, "I have heard that the superior man is not a partisan. May the superior man be a partisan also? The prince married a daughter of the house of WU, of the same surname with himself, and called her—'The elder Tsze of Wu.' If the prince knew propriety, who does not know it?"

Wu-ma Ch'i reported these remarks, and the Master said, "I am fortunate! If I have any errors, people are sure to know them."

When the Master was in company with a person who was singing, if he sang well, he would make him repeat the song, while he accompanied it with his own voice.

The Master said, "In letters I am perhaps equal to other men, but the character of the superior man, carrying out in his conduct what he professes, is what I have not yet attained to."

The Master said, "The sage and the man of perfect virtue—how dare I rank myself with them? It may simply be said of me, that I strive to become such without satiety, and teach others without weariness." Kung-hsi Hwa said, "This is just what we, the disciples, cannot imitate you in."

The Master being very sick, Tsze-lu asked leave to pray for him. He said, "May such a thing be done?" Tsze-lu replied, "It may. In the Eulogies it is said, 'Prayer has been made for thee to the spirits of the upper and lower worlds.'" The Master said, "My praying has been for a long time."

The Master said, "Extravagance leads to insubordination, and parsimony to meanness. It is better to be mean than to be insubordinate."

The Master said, "The superior man is satisfied and composed; the mean man is always full of distress."

The Master was mild, and yet dignified; majestic, and yet not fierce; respectful, and yet easy.

8

THE MASTER said, "T'ai-po may be said to have reached the highest point of virtuous action. Thrice he declined the kingdom, and the people in ignorance of his motives could not express their approbation of his conduct."

The Master said, "Respectfulness, without the rules of propriety, becomes laborious bustle; carefulness, without the rules of propriety, becomes timidity; boldness, without the rules of propriety, becomes insubordination; straightforwardness, without the rules of propriety, becomes rudeness.

"When those who are in high stations perform well all their duties to their relations, the people are aroused to virtue. When old friends are not neglected by them, the people are preserved from meanness."

The philosopher Tsang being ill, he cared to him the disciples of his school, and said, "Uncover my feet, uncover my hands. It is said in the Book of Poetry, 'We should be apprehensive and cautious, as if on the brink of a deep gulf, as if treading on thin ice,' and so have I been. Now and hereafter, I know my escape from all injury to my person. O ye, my little children."

The philosopher Tsang being ill, Meng Chang went to ask how he was.

Tsang said to him, "When a bird is about to die, its notes are mournful; when a man is about to die, his words are good.

"There are three principles of conduct which the man of high rank should consider specially important—that in his deportment and manner he keep from violence and heedlessness; that in regulating his countenance he keep near to sincerity; and that in his words and tones he keep far from lowness and impropriety. As to such matters as attending to the sacrificial vessels, there are the proper officers for them."

The philosopher Tsang said, "Gifted with ability, and yet putting questions to those who were not so; possessed of much, and yet putting questions to those possessed of little; having, as though he had not; full, and yet counting himself as empty; offended against, and yet entering into no altercation; formerly I had a friend who pursued this style of conduct."

The philosopher Tsang said, "Suppose that there is an individual who can be entrusted with the charge of a young orphan prince, and can be commissioned with authority over a state of a hundred li, and whom no emergency however great can drive from his principles—is such a man a superior man? He is a superior man indeed."

The philosopher Tsang said, "The officer may not be without breadth of mind and vigorous endurance. His burden is heavy and his course is long.

"Perfect virtue is the burden which he considers it is his to sustain—is it not heavy? Only with death does his course stop—is it not long?"

The Master said, "It is by the Odes that the mind is aroused.

"It is by the Rules of Propriety that the character is established.

"It is from Music that the finish is received."

The Master said, "The people may be made to follow a path of action, but they may not be made to understand it."

The Master said, "The man who is fond of daring and is dissatisfied with poverty, will proceed to insubordination. So will the man who is not virtuous, when you carry your dislike of him to an extreme."

The Master said, "Though a man have abilities as admirable as those of the Duke of Chau, yet if he be proud and niggardly, those other things are really not worth being looked at."

The Master said, "It is not easy to find a man who has learned for three years without coming to be good."

The Master said, "With sincere faith he unites the love of learning; holding firm to death, he is perfecting the excellence of his course.

"Such a one will not enter a tottering state, nor dwell in a disorganized one. When right principles of government prevail in the kingdom, he will show himself; when they are prostrated, he will keep concealed.

"When a country is well governed, poverty and a mean condition are things to be ashamed of. When a country is ill governed, riches and honor are things to be ashamed of."

The Master said, "He who is not in any particular office has nothing to do with plans for the administration of its duties."

The Master said, "When the music master Chih first entered on his office, the finish of the Kwan Tsu was magnificent—how it filled the ears!"

The Master said, "Ardent and yet not upright, stupid and yet not attentive; simple and yet not sincere—such persons I do not understand."

The Master said, "Learn as if you could not reach your object, and were always fearing also lest you should lose it."

The Master said, "How majestic was the manner in which Shun and Yu held possession of the empire, as if it were nothing to them!"

The Master said, "Great indeed was Yao as a sovereign! How majestic was he! It is only Heaven that is grand, and only Yao corresponded to it. How vast was his virtue! The people could find no name for it.

"How majestic was he in the works which he accomplished! How glorious in the elegant regulations which he instituted!"

Shun had five ministers, and the empire was well governed.

King Wu said, "I have ten able ministers."

Confucius said, "Is not the saying that talents are difficult to find, true? Only when the dynasties of T'ang and Yu met, were they more abundant than in this of Chau, yet there was a woman among them. The able ministers were no more than nine men.

"King Wan possessed two of the three parts of the empire, and with those he served the dynasty of Yin. The virtue of the house of Chau may be said to have reached the highest point indeed."

The Master said, "I can find no flaw in the character of Yu. He used himself coarse food and drink, but displayed the utmost filial piety towards the spirits. His ordinary garments were poor, but he displayed the utmost elegance in his sacrificial cap and apron. He lived in a low, mean house, but expended all his strength on the ditches and water channels. I can find nothing like a flaw in Yu."

9

THE SUBJECTS of which the Master seldom spoke were—profitableness, and also the appointments of Heaven, and perfect virtue.

A man of the village of Ta-hsiang said, "Great indeed is the philosopher K'ung! His learning is extensive, and yet he does not render his name famous by any particular thing."

The Master heard the observation, and said to his disciples, "What shall I practice? Shall I practice charioteering, or shall I practice archery? I will practice charioteering."

The Master said, "The linen cap is that prescribed by the rules of ceremony, but now a silk one is worn. It is economical, and I follow the common practice.

"The rules of ceremony prescribe the bowing below the hall, but now the practice is to bow only after ascending it. That is arrogant. I continue to bow below the hall, though I oppose the common practice."

There were four things from which the Master was entirely free. He had no foregone conclusions, no arbitrary predeterminations, no obstinacy, and no egoism.

The Master was put in fear in K'wang.

He said, "After the death of King Wan, was not the cause of truth lodged here in me?

"If Heaven had wished to let this cause of truth perish, then I, a future mortal! should not have got such a relation to that cause. While Heaven does not let the cause of truth perish, what can the people of K'wang do to me?"

A high officer asked Tsze-kung, saying, "May we not say that your Master is a sage? How various is his ability!"

Tsze-kung said, "Certainly Heaven has endowed him unlimitedly. He is about a sage. And, moreover, his ability is various."

The Master heard of the conversation and said, "Does the high officer know me? When I was young, my condition was low, and I acquired my ability in many things, but they were mean matters. Must the superior man have such variety of ability? He does not need variety of ability." Lao said, "The Master said, 'Having no official employment, I acquired many arts.'"

The Master said, "Am I indeed possessed of knowledge? I am not knowing. But if a mean person, who appears quite empty-like, ask anything of me, I set it forth from one end to the other, and exhaust it."

The Master said, "The Fang bird does not come; the river sends forth no map—it is all over with me!"

When the Master saw a person in a mourning dress, or any one with the cap and upper and lower garments of full dress, or a blind person, on observing them approaching, though they were younger than himself, he would rise up, and if he had to pass by them, he would do so hastily.

Yen Yuan, in admiration of the Master's doctrines, sighed and said, "I looked up to them, and they seemed to become more high; I tried to penetrate them, and they seemed to become more firm; I looked at them before me, and suddenly they seemed to be behind.

"The Master, by orderly method, skillfully leads men on. He enlarged my mind with learning, and taught me the restraints of propriety.

"When I wish to give over the study of his doctrines, I cannot do so, and having exerted all my ability, there seems something to stand right up before me; but though I wish to follow and lay hold of it, I really find no way to do so."

The Master being very ill, Tsze-lu wished the disciples to act as ministers to him.

During a remission of his illness, he said, "Long has the conduct of Yu been deceitful! By pretending to have ministers when I have them not, whom should I impose upon? Should I impose upon Heaven?

"Moreover, than that I should die in the hands of ministers, is it not better that I should die in the hands of you, my disciples? And though I may not get a great burial, shall I die upon the road?"

Tsze-kung said, "There is a beautiful gem here. Should I lay it up in a case and keep it? or should I seek for a good price and sell it?" The Master said, "Sell it! Sell it! But I would wait for one to offer the price."

The Master was wishing to go and live among the nine wild tribes of the east.

Some one said, "They are rude. How can you do such a thing?" The Master said, "If a superior man dwelt among them, what rudeness would there be?"

The Master said, "I returned from Wei to Lu, and then the music was reformed, and the pieces in the Royal songs and Praise songs all found their proper places."

The Master said, "Abroad, to serve the high ministers and nobles; at home, to serve one's father and elder brothers; in all duties to the dead, not to dare not to exert one's self; and not to be overcome of wine—which one of these things do I attain to?"

The Master standing by a stream, said, "It passes on just like this, not ceasing day or night!"

The Master said, "I have not seen one who loves virtue as he loves beauty."

The Master said, "The prosecution of learning may be compared to what may happen in raising a mound. If there want but one basket of earth to complete the work, and I stop, the stopping is my own work. It may be compared to throwing down the earth on the level ground. Though but one basketful is thrown at a time, the advancing with it my own going forward."

The Master said, "Never flagging when I set forth anything to him—ah! that is Hui." The Master said of Yen Yuan, "Alas! I saw his constant advance. I never saw him stop in his progress."

The Master said, "There are cases in which the blade springs, but the plant does not go on to flower! There are cases where it flowers but fruit is not subsequently produced!"

The Master said, "A youth is to be regarded with respect. How do we know that his future will not be equal to our present? If he reach the age of forty or fifty, and has not made himself heard of, then indeed he will not be worth being regarded with respect."

The Master said, "Can men refuse to assent to the words of strict admonition? But it is reforming the conduct because of them which is valuable. Can men refuse to be pleased with words of gentle advice? But it is unfolding their aim which is valuable. If a man be pleased with these words, but does not unfold their aim, and assents to those, but does not reform his conduct, I can really do nothing with him."

The Master said, "Hold faithfulness and sincerity as first principles. Have no friends not equal to yourself. When you have faults, do not fear to abandon them."

The Master said, "The commander of the forces of a large state may be carried off, but the will of even a common man cannot be taken from him."

The Master said, "Dressed himself in a tattered robe quilted with hemp, yet standing by the side of men dressed in furs, and not ashamed—ah! it is Yu who is equal to this!

"He dislikes none, he covets nothing—what can he do but what is good!"

Tsze-lu kept continually repeating these words of the ode, when the Master said, "Those things are by no means sufficient to constitute perfect excellence."

The Master said, "When the year becomes cold, then we know how the pine and the cypress are the last to lose their leaves."

The Master said, "The wise are free from perplexities; the virtuous from anxiety; and the bold from fear."

The Master said, "There are some with whom we may study in common, but we shall find them unable to go along with us to principles. Perhaps we may go on with them to principles, but we shall find them unable to get established in those along with us. Or if we may get so established along with them, we shall find them unable to weigh occurring events along with us."

"How the flowers of the aspen-plum flutter and turn! Do I not think of you? But your house is distant."

The Master said, "It is the want of thought about it. How is it distant?"

10

CONFUCIUS, in his village, looked simple and sincere, and as if he were not able to speak.

When he was in the prince's ancestral temple, or in the court, he spoke minutely on every point, but cautiously.

When he was waiting at court, in speaking with the great officers of the lower grade, he spoke freely, but in a straightforward manner; in speaking with those of the higher grade, he did so blandly, but precisely.

When the ruler was present, his manner displayed respectful uneasiness; it was grave, but self-possessed.

When the prince called him to employ him in the reception of a visitor, his countenance appeared to change, and his legs to move forward with difficulty.

He inclined himself to the other officers among whom he stood, moving his left or right arm, as their position required, but keeping the skirts of his robe before and behind evenly adjusted.

He hastened forward, with his arms like the wings of a bird.

When the guest had retired, he would report to the prince, "The visitor is not turning round any more."

When he entered the palace gate, he seemed to bend his body, as if it were not sufficient to admit him.

When he was standing, he did not occupy the middle of the gateway; when he passed in or out, he did not tread upon the threshold.

When he was passing the vacant place of the prince, his countenance appeared to change, and his legs to bend under him, and his words came as if he hardly had breath to utter them.

He ascended the reception hall, holding up his robe with both his hands, and his body bent; holding in his breath also, as if he dared not breathe.

When he came out from the audience, as soon as he had descended one step, he began to relax his countenance, and had a satisfied look. When he had got the bottom of the steps, he advanced rapidly to his place, with his arms like wings, and on occupying it, his manner still showed respectful uneasiness.

When he was carrying the scepter of his ruler, he seemed to bend his body, as if he were not able to bear its weight. He did not hold it higher than the position of the hands in making a bow, nor lower than their position in giving anything to another. His countenance seemed to change, and look apprehensive, and he dragged his feet along as if they were held by something to the ground.

In presenting the presents with which he was charged, he wore a placid appearance.

At his private audience, he looked highly pleased.

The superior man did not use a deep purple, or a puce color, in the ornaments of his dress.

Even in his undress, he did not wear anything of a red or reddish color.

In warm weather, he had a single garment either of coarse or fine texture, but he wore it displayed over an inner garment.

Over lamb's fur he wore a garment of black; over fawn's fur one of white; and over fox's fur one of yellow.

The fur robe of his undress was long, with the right sleeve short.

He required his sleeping dress to be half as long again as his body.

When staying at home, he used thick furs of the fox or the badger.

When he put off mourning, he wore all the appendages of the girdle.

His undergarment, except when it was required to be of the curtain shape, was made of silk cut narrow above and wide below.

He did not wear lamb's fur or a black cap on a visit of condolence.

On the first day of the month he put on his court robes, and presented himself at court.

When fasting, he thought it necessary to have his clothes brightly clean and made of linen cloth.

When fasting, he thought it necessary to change his food, and also to change the place where he commonly sat in the apartment.

He did not dislike to have his rice finely cleaned, nor to have his mince meat cut quite small.

He did not eat rice which had been injured by heat or damp and turned sour, nor fish or flesh which was gone. He did not eat what was discolored, or what was of a bad flavor, nor anything which was ill-cooked, or was not in season.

He did not eat meat which was not cut properly, nor what was served without its proper sauce.

Though there might be a large quantity of meat, he would not allow what he took to exceed the due proportion for the rice. It was only in wine that he laid down no limit for himself, but he did not allow himself to be confused by it.

He did not partake of wine and dried meat bought in the market.

He was never without ginger when he ate. He did not eat much.

When he had been assisting at the prince's sacrifice, he did not keep the flesh which he received overnight. The flesh of his family sacrifice he did not keep over three days. If kept over three days, people could not eat it.

When eating, he did not converse. When in bed, he did not speak.

Although his food might be coarse rice and vegetable soup, he would offer a little of it in sacrifice with a grave, respectful air.

If his mat was not straight, he did not sit on it.

When the villagers were drinking together, upon those who carried staffs going out, he also went out immediately after.

When the villagers were going through their ceremonies to drive away pestilential influences, he put on his court robes and stood on the eastern steps.

When he was sending complimentary inquiries to any one in another state, he bowed twice as he escorted the messenger away.

Chi K'ang having sent him a present of physic, he bowed and received it, saying, "I do not know it. I dare not taste it."

The stable being burned down, when he was at court, on his return he said, "Has any man been hurt?" He did not ask about the horses.

When the he would adjust his mat, first taste it, and then give it away to others. When the prince sent him a gift of undressed meat, he would have it cooked, and offer it to the spirits of his ancestors. When the prince sent him a gift of a living animal, he would keep it alive.

When he was in attendance on the prince and joining in the entertainment, the prince only sacrificed. He first tasted everything.

When he was ill and the prince came to visit him, he had his head to the east, made his court robes be spread over him, and drew his girdle across them.

When the prince's order called him, without waiting for his carriage to be yoked, he went at once.

When he entered the ancestral temple of the state, he asked about everything.

When any of his friends died, if he had no relations offices, he would say, "I will bury him."

When a friend sent him a present, though it might be a carriage and horses, he did not bow.

The only present for which he bowed was that of the flesh of sacrifice.

In bed, he did not lie like a corpse. At home, he did not put on any formal deportment.

When he saw any one in a mourning dress, though it might be an acquaintance, he would change countenance; when he saw any one wearing the cap of full dress, or a blind person, though he might be in his undress, he would salute him in a ceremonious manner.

To any person in mourning he bowed forward to the crossbar of his carriage; he bowed in the same way to any one bearing the tables of population.

When he was at an entertainment where there was an abundance of provisions set before him, he would change countenance and rise up.

On a sudden clap of thunder, or a violent wind, he would change countenance.

When he was about to mount his carriage, he would stand straight, holding the cord.

When he was in the carriage, he did not turn his head quite round, he did not talk hastily, he did not point with his hands.

Seeing the countenance, it instantly rises. It flies round, and by and by settles.

The Master said, "There is the hen-pheasant on the hill bridge. At its season! At its season!" Tsze-lu made a motion to it. Thrice it smelt him and then rose.

11

THE MASTER said, "The men of former times in the matters of ceremonies and music were rustics, it is said, while the men of these latter times, in ceremonies and music, are accomplished gentlemen.

"If I have occasion to use those things, I follow the men of former times."

The Master said, "Of those who were with me in Ch'an and Ts'ai, there are none to be found to enter my door."

Distinguished for their virtuous principles and practice, there were Yen Yuan, Min Tsze-ch'ien, Zan Po-niu, and Chung-kung; for their ability in speech, Tsai Wo and Tsze-kung; for their administrative talents, Zan Yu and Chi Lu; for their literary acquirements, Tsze-yu and Tsze-hsia.

The Master said, "Hui gives me no assistance. There is nothing that I say in which he does not delight."

The Master said, "Filial indeed is Min Tsze-ch'ien! Other people say nothing of him different from the report of his parents and brothers."

Nan Yung was frequently repeating the lines about a white scepter stone. Confucius gave him the daughter of his elder brother to wife.

Chi K'ang asked which of the disciples loved to learn. Confucius replied to him, "There was Yen Hui; he loved to learn. Unfortunately his appointed time was short, and he died. Now there is no one who loves to learn, as he did."

When Yen Yuan died, Yen Lu begged the carriage of the Master to sell and get an outer shell for his son's coffin.

The Master said, "Every one calls his son his son, whether he has talents or has not talents. There was Li; when he died, he had a coffin but no outer shell. I would not walk on foot to get a shell for him, because, having followed in the rear of the great officers, it was not proper that I should walk on foot."

When Yen Yuan died, the Master said, "Alas! Heaven is destroying me! Heaven is destroying me!"

When Yen Yuan died, the Master bewailed him exceedingly, and the disciples who were with him said, "Master, your grief is excessive!"

"Is it excessive?" said he. "If I am not to mourn bitterly for this man, for whom should I mourn?"

When Yen Yuan died, the disciples wished to give him a great funeral, and the Master said, "You may not do so."

The disciples did bury him in great style.

The Master said, "Hui behaved towards me as his father. I have not been able to treat him as my son. The fault is not mine; it belongs to you, O disciples."

Chi Lu asked about serving the spirits of the dead. The Master said, "While you are not able to serve men, how can you serve their spirits?" Chi Lu added, "I venture to ask about death?" He was answered, "While you do not know life, how can you know about death?"

The disciple Min was standing by his side, looking bland and precise; Tsze-lu, looking bold and soldierly; Zan Yu and Tsze-kung, with a free and straightforward manner. The Master was pleased.

He said, "Yu, there!—he will not die a natural death."

Some parties in Lu were going to take down and rebuild the Long Treasury.

Min Tsze-ch'ien said, "Suppose it were to be repaired after its old style—why must it be altered and made anew?"

The Master said, "This man seldom speaks; when he does, he is sure to hit the point."

The Master said, "What has the lute of Yu to do in my door?"

The other disciples began not to respect Tszelu. The Master said, "Yu has ascended to the hall, though he has not yet passed into the inner apartments."

Tsze-kung asked which of the two, Shih or Shang, was the superior. The Master said, "Shih goes beyond the due mean, and Shang does not come up to it."

"Then," said Tsze-kung, "the superiority is with Shih, I suppose."

The Master said, "To go beyond is as wrong as to fall short."

The head of the Chi family was richer than the duke of Chau had been, and yet Ch'iu collected his imposts for him, and increased his wealth.

The Master said, "He is no disciple of mine. My little children, beat the drum and assail him."

Ch'ai is simple. Shan is dull. Shih is specious. Yu is coarse.

The Master said, "There is Hui! He has nearly attained to perfect virtue. He is often in want.

"Ts'ze does not acquiesce in the appointments of Heaven, and his goods are increased by him. Yet his judgments are often correct."

Tsze-chang asked what were the characteristics of the good man.

The Master said, "He does not tread in the footsteps of others, but moreover, he does not enter the chamber of the sage."

The Master said, "If, because a man's discourse appears solid and sincere, we allow him to be a good man, is he really a superior man? or is his gravity only in appearance?"

Tsze-lu asked whether he should immediately carry into practice what he heard. The Master said, "There are your father and elder brothers to be consulted—why should you act on that principle of immediately carrying into practice what you hear?" Zan Yu asked the same, whether he should immediately carry into practice what he heard, and the Master answered, "Immediately carry into practice what you hear." Kung-hsi Hwa said, "Yu asked whether he should carry immediately into practice what he heard, and you said, 'There are your father and elder brothers to be consulted.' Ch'iu asked whether he should immediately carry into practice what he heard, and you said, 'Carry it immediately into practice.' I, Ch'ih, am perplexed, and venture to ask you for an explanation." The Master said, "Ch'iu is retiring and slow; therefore I urged him forward. Yu has more than his own share of energy; therefore I kept him back."

The Master was put in fear in K'wang and Yen Yuan fell behind. The Master, on his rejoining him, said, "I thought you had died." Hui replied, "While you were alive, how should I presume to die?"

Chi Tsze-zan asked whether Chung Yu and Zan Ch'iu could be called great ministers.

The Master said, "I thought you would ask about some extraordinary individuals, and you only ask about Yu and Ch'iu!

"What is called a great minister, is one who serves his prince according to what is right, and when he finds he cannot do so, retires.

"Now, as to Yu and Ch'iu, they may be called ordinary ministers."

Tsze-zan said, "Then they will always follow their chief—win they?"

The Master said, "In an act of parricide or regicide, they would not follow him."

Tsze-lu got Tsze-kao appointed governor of Pi.

The Master said, "You are injuring a man's son."

Tsze-lu said, "There are, there, common people and officers; there are the altars of the spirits of the land and grain. Why must one read books before he can be considered to have learned?"

The Master said, "It is on this account that I hate your glib-tongued people."

Tsze-lu, Tsang Hsi, Zan Yu, and Kunghsi Hwa were sitting by the Master.

He said to them, "Though I am a day or so older than you, do not think of that.

"From day to day you are saying, 'We are not known.' If some ruler were to know you, what would you like to do?"

Tsze-lu hastily and lightly replied, "Suppose the case of a state of ten thousand chariots; let it be straitened between other large cities; let it be suffering from invading armies; and to this let there be added a famine in corn and in all vegetables—if I were intrusted with the government of it, in three years' time I could make the people to be bold, and to recognize the rules of righteous conduct." The Master smiled at him.

Turning to Yen Yu, he said, "Ch'iu, what are your wishes?" Ch'iu replied, "Suppose a state of sixty or seventy li square, or one of fifty or sixty, and let me have the government of it—in three years' time, I could make plenty to abound among the people. As to teaching them the principles of propriety, and music, I must wait for the rise of a superior man to do that."

"What are your wishes, Ch'ih," said the Master next to Kung-hsi Hwa. Ch'ih replied, "I do not say that my ability extends to these things, but I should wish to learn them. At the services of the ancestral temple, and at the audiences of the princes with the sovereign, I should like, dressed in the dark square-made robe and the black linen cap, to act as a small assistant."

Last of all, the Master asked Tsang Hsi, "Tien, what are your wishes?" Tien, pausing as he was playing on his lute, while it was yet twanging, laid the instrument aside, and "My wishes," he said, "are different from the cherished purposes of these three gentlemen." "What harm is there in that?" said the Master; "do you also, as well as they, speak out your wishes." Tien then said, "In this, the last month of spring, with the dress of the season all complete, along with five or six young men who have assumed the cap, and six or seven boys, I would wash in the I, enjoy the breeze among the rain altars, and return home singing." The Master heaved a sigh and said, "I give my approval to Tien."

The three others having gone out, Tsang Hsi remained behind, and said, "What do you think of the words of these three friends?" The Master replied, "They simply told each one his wishes."

Hsi pursued, "Master, why did you smile at Yu?"

He was answered, "The management of a state demands the rules of propriety. His words were not humble; therefore I smiled at him."

Hsi again said, "But was it not a state which Ch'iu proposed for himself?" The reply was, "Yes; did you ever see a territory of sixty or seventy li or one of fifty or sixty, which was not a state?"

Once more, Hsi inquired, "And was it not a state which Ch'ih proposed for himself?" The Master again replied, "Yes; who but princes have to do with ancestral temples, and with audiences but the sovereign? If Ch'ih were to be a small assistant in these services, who could be a great one?"

12

YEN YUAN asked about perfect virtue. The Master said, "To subdue one's self and return to propriety, is perfect virtue. If a man can for one day subdue himself and return to propriety, an under heaven will ascribe perfect virtue to him. Is the practice of perfect virtue from a man himself, or is it from others?"

Yen Yuan said, "I beg to ask the steps of that process." The Master replied, "Look not at what is contrary to propriety; listen not to what is contrary to propriety; speak not what is contrary to propriety; make no movement which is contrary to propriety." Yen Yuan then said, "Though I am deficient in intelligence and vigor, I will make it my business to practice this lesson."

Chung-kung asked about perfect virtue. The Master said, "It is, when you go abroad, to behave to every one as if you were receiving a great guest; to employ the people as if you were assisting at a great sacrifice; not to do to others as you would not wish done to yourself; to have no murmuring against you in the country, and none in the family." Chung-kung said, "Though I am deficient in intelligence and vigor, I will make it my business to practice this lesson."

Sze-ma Niu asked about perfect virtue.

The Master said, "The man of perfect virtue is cautious and slow in his speech."

"Cautious and slow in his speech!" said Niu—"is this what is meant by perfect virtue?" The Master said, "When a man feels the difficulty of doing, can he be other than cautious and slow in speaking?"

Sze-ma Niu asked about the superior man. The Master said, "The superior man has neither anxiety nor fear."

"Being without anxiety or fear!" said Nui; "does this constitute what we call the superior man?"

The Master said, "When internal examination discovers nothing wrong, what is there to be anxious about, what is there to fear?"

Sze-ma Niu, full of anxiety, said, "Other men all have their brothers, I only have not."

Tsze-hsia said to him, "There is the following saying which I have heard—'Death and life have their determined appointment; riches and honors depend upon Heaven.'

"Let the superior man never fail reverentially to order his own conduct, and let him be respectful to others and observant of propriety—

then all within the four seas will be his brothers. What has the superior man to do with being distressed because he has no brothers?"

Tsze-chang asked what constituted intelligence. The Master said, "He with whom neither slander that gradually soaks into the mind, nor statements that startle like a wound in the flesh, are successful may be called intelligent indeed. Yea, he with whom neither soaking slander, nor startling statements, are successful, may be called farseeing."

Tsze-kung asked about government. The Master said, "The requisites of government are that there be sufficiency of food, sufficiency of military equipment, and the confidence of the people in their ruler."

Tsze-kung said, "If it cannot be helped, and one of these must be dispensed with, which of the three should be foregone first?" "The military equipment," said the Master.

Tsze-kung again asked, "If it cannot be helped, and one of the remaining two must be dispensed with, which of them should be foregone?" The Master answered, "Part with the food. From of old, death has been the lot of men; but if the people have no faith in their rulers, there is no standing for the state."

Chi Tsze-ch'ang said, "In a superior man it is only the substantial qualities which are wanted—why should we seek for ornamental accomplishments?"

Tsze-kung said, "Alas! Your words, sir, show you to be a superior man, but four horses cannot overtake the tongue. Ornament is as substance; substance is as ornament. The hide of a tiger or a leopard stripped of its hair, is like the hide of a dog or a goat stripped of its hair."

The Duke Ai inquired of Yu Zo, saying, "The year is one of scarcity, and the returns for expenditure are not sufficient—what is to be done?"

Yu Zo replied to him, "Why not simply tithe the people?"

"With two tenths," said the duke, "I find it not enough—how could I do with that system of one tenth?"

Yu Zo answered, "If the people have plenty, their prince will not be left to want alone. If the people are in want, their prince cannot enjoy plenty alone."

Tsze-chang having asked how virtue was to be exalted, and delusions to be discovered, the Master said, "Hold faithfulness and sincerity as first principles, and be moving continually to what is right—this is the way to exalt one's virtue.

"You love a man and wish him to live; you hate him and wish him to die. Having wished him to live, you also wish him to die. This is a case of delusion. 'It may not be on account of her being rich, yet you come to make a difference.'"

The Duke Ching, of Ch'i, asked Confucius about government. Confucius replied, "There is government, when the prince is prince, and the minister is minister; when the father is father, and the son is son."

"Good!" said the duke; "if, indeed, the prince be not prince, the not minister, the father not father, and the son not son, although I have my revenue, can I enjoy it?"

The Master said, "Ah! it is Yu, who could with half a word settle litigations!"

Tsze-lu never slept over a promise.

The Master said, "In hearing litigations, I am like any other body. What is necessary, however, is to cause the people to have no litigations."

Tsze-chang asked about government. The Master said, "The art of governing is to keep its affairs before the mind without weariness, and to practice them with undeviating consistency."

The Master said, "By extensively studying all learning, and keeping himself under the restraint of the rules of propriety, one may thus likewise not err from what is right."

The Master said, "The superior man seeks to perfect the admirable qualities of men, and does not seek to perfect their bad qualities. The mean man does the opposite of this."

Chi K'ang asked Confucius about government. Confucius replied, "To govern means to rectify. If you lead on the people with correctness, who will dare not to be correct?"

Chi K'ang, distressed about the number of thieves in the state, inquired of Confucius how to do away with them. Confucius said, "If you, sir, were not covetous, although you should reward them to do it, they would not steal."

Chi K'ang asked Confucius about government, saying, "What do you say to killing the unprincipled for the good of the principled?" Confucius replied, "Sir, in carrying on your government, why should you use killing at all? Let your evinced desires be for what is good, and the people will be good. The relation between superiors and inferiors is like that between the wind and the grass. The grass must bend, when the wind blows across it."

Tsze-chang asked, "What must the officer be, who may be said to be distinguished?"

The Master said, "What is it you call being distinguished?"

Tsze-chang replied, "It is to be heard of through the state, to be heard of throughout his clan."

The Master said, "That is notoriety, not distinction.

"Now the man of distinction is solid and straightforward, and loves righteousness. He examines people's words, and looks at their countenances. He is anxious to humble himself to others. Such a man will be distinguished in the country; he will be distinguished in his clan.

"As to the man of notoriety, he assumes the appearance of virtue, but his actions are opposed to it, and he rests in this character without any doubts about himself. Such a man will be heard of in the country; he will be heard of in the clan."

Fan Ch'ih rambling with the Master under the trees about the rain altars, said, "I venture to ask how to exalt virtue, to correct cherished evil, and to discover delusions."

The Master said, "Truly a good question!

"If doing what is to be done be made the first business, and success a secondary consideration—is not this the way to exalt virtue? To assail one's own wickedness and not assail that of others—is not this the way to correct cherished evil? For a morning's anger to disregard one's own life, and involve that of his parents—is not this a case of delusion?"

Fan Ch'ih asked about benevolence. The Master said, "It is to love all men." He asked about knowledge. The Master said, "It is to know all men."

Fan Ch'ih did not immediately understand these answers.

The Master said, "Employ the upright and put aside all the crooked; in this way the crooked can be made to be upright."

Fan Ch'ih retired, and, seeing Tsze-hsia, he said to him, "A little while ago, I had an interview with our Master, and asked him about knowledge. He said, 'Employ the upright, and put aside all the crooked— in this way, the crooked will be made to be upright.' What did he mean?"

Tsze-hsia said, "Truly rich is his saying!

"Shun, being in possession of the kingdom, selected from among all the people, and employed Kai-yao—on which all who were devoid of virtue disappeared. T'ang, being in possession of the kingdom, selected from among all the people, and employed I Yin—and all who were devoid of virtue disappeared."

Tsze-kung asked about friendship. The Master said, "Faithfully admonish your friend, and skillfully lead him on. If you find him impracticable, stop. Do not disgrace yourself."

The philosopher Tsang said, "The superior man on grounds of culture meets with his friends, and by friendship helps his virtue."

13

TSZE-LU ASKED about government. The Master said, "Go before the people with your example, and be laborious in their affairs."

He requested further instruction, and was answered, "Be not weary in these things."

Chung-kung, being chief minister to the head of the Chi family, asked about government. The Master said, "Employ first the services of your various officers, pardon small faults, and raise to office men of virtue and talents."

Chung-kung said, "How shall I know the men of virtue and talent, so that I may raise them to office?" He was answered, "Raise to office those whom you know. As to those whom you do not know, will others neglect them?"

Tsze-lu said, "The ruler of Wei has been waiting for you, in order with you to administer the government. What will you consider the first thing to be done?"

The Master replied, "What is necessary is to rectify names."

"So! indeed!" said Tsze-lu. "You are wide of the mark! Why must there be such rectification?"

The Master said, "How uncultivated you are, Yu! A superior man, in regard to what he does not know, shows a cautious reserve.

"If names be not correct, language is not in accordance with the truth of things. If language be not in accordance with the truth of things, affairs cannot be carried on to success.

"When affairs cannot be carried on to success, proprieties and music do not flourish. When proprieties and music do not flourish, punishments will not be properly awarded. When punishments are not properly awarded, the people do not know how to move hand or foot.

"Therefore a superior man considers it necessary that the names he uses may be spoken appropriately, and also that what he speaks may be carried out appropriately. What the superior man requires is just that in his words there may be nothing incorrect."

Fan Ch'ih requested to be taught husbandry. The Master said, "I am not so good for that as an old husbandman." He requested also to be taught gardening, and was answered, "I am not so good for that as an old gardener."

Fan Ch'ih having gone out, the Master said, "A small man, indeed, is Fan Hsu! If a superior man love propriety, the people will not dare not to be reverent. If he love righteousness, the people will not dare not to submit to his example. If he love good faith, the people will not dare not to be sincere. Now, when these things obtain, the people from all quarters will come to him, bearing their children on their backs; what need has he of a knowledge of husbandry?"

The Master said, "Though a man may be able to recite the three hundred odes, yet if, when intrusted with a governmental charge, he knows not how to act, or if, when sent to any quarter on a mission, he cannot give his replies unassisted, notwithstanding the extent of his learning, of what practical use is it?"

The Master said, "When a prince's personal conduct is correct, his government is effective without the issuing of orders. If his personal conduct is not correct, he may issue orders, but they will not be followed."

The Master said, "The governments of Lu and Wei are brothers."

The Master said of Ching, a scion of the ducal family of Wei, that he knew the economy of a family well. When he began to have means, he said, "Ha! here is a collection!" When they were a little increased, he said, "Ha! this is complete!" When he had become rich, he said, "Ha! this is admirable!"

When the Master went to Wei! Zan Yu acted as driver of his carriage.

The Master observed, "How numerous are the people!"

Yu said, "Since they are thus numerous, what more shall be done for them?" "Enrich them," was the reply.

"And when they have been enriched, what more shall be done?" The Master said, "Teach them."

The Master said, "If there were any of the princes who would employ me, in the course of twelve months, I should have done something considerable. In three years, the government would be perfected."

The Master said, "'If good men were to govern a country in succession for a hundred years, they would be able to transform the violently

---

41

bad, and dispense with capital punishments.' True indeed is this saying!"

The Master said, "If a truly royal ruler were to arise, it would stir require a generation, and then virtue would prevail."

The Master said, "If a minister make his own conduct correct, what difficulty will he have in assisting in government? If he cannot rectify himself, what has he to do with rectifying others?"

The disciple Zan returning from the court, the Master said to him, "How are you so late?" He replied, "We had government business." The Master said, "It must have been family affairs. If there had been government business, though I am not now in office, I should have been consulted about it."

The Duke Ting asked whether there was a single sentence which could make a country prosperous. Confucius replied, "Such an effect cannot be expected from one sentence.

"There is a saying, however, which people have—'To be a prince is difficult; to be a minister is not easy.'

"If a ruler knows this—the difficulty of being a prince—may there not be expected from this one sentence the prosperity of his country?"

The duke then said, "Is there a single sentence which can ruin a country?" Confucius replied, "Such an effect as that cannot be expected from one sentence. There is, however, the saying which people have—'I have no pleasure in being a prince, but only in that no one can offer any opposition to what I say!'

"If a ruler's words be good, is it not also good that no one oppose them? But if they are not good, and no one opposes them, may there not be expected from this one sentence the ruin of his country?"

The Duke of Sheh asked about government.

The Master said, "Good government obtains when those who are near are made happy, and those who are far off are attracted."

Tsze-hsia, being governor of Chu-fu, asked about government. The Master said, "Do not be desirous to have things done quickly; do not look at small advantages. Desire to have things done quickly prevents their being done thoroughly. Looking at small advantages prevents great affairs from being accomplished."

The Duke of Sheh informed Confucius, saying, "Among us here there are those who may be styled upright in their conduct. If their father have stolen a sheep, they will bear witness to the fact."

Confucius said, "Among us, in our part of the country, those who are upright are different from this. The father conceals the misconduct of the son, and the son conceals the misconduct of the father. Uprightness is to be found in this."

Fan Ch'ih asked about perfect virtue. The Master said, "It is, in retirement, to be sedately grave; in the management of business, to be reverently attentive; in intercourse with others, to be strictly sincere. Though a man go among rude, uncultivated tribes, these qualities may not be neglected."

Tsze-kung asked, saying, "What qualities must a man possess to entitle him to be called an officer?" The Master said, "He who in his conduct of himself maintains a sense of shame, and when sent to any quarter will not disgrace his prince's commission, deserves to be called an officer."

Tsze-kung pursued, "I venture to ask who may be placed in the next lower rank?" And he was told, "He whom the circle of his relatives pronounce to be filial, whom his fellow villagers and neighbors pronounce to be fraternal."

Again the disciple asked, "I venture to ask about the class still next in order." The Master said, "They are determined to be sincere in what they say, and to carry out what they do. They are obstinate little men. Yet perhaps they may make the next class."

Tsze-kung finally inquired, "Of what sort are those of the present day, who engage in government?" The Master said, "Pooh! they are so many pecks and hampers, not worth being taken into account."

The Master said, "Since I cannot get men pursuing the due medium, to whom I might communicate my instructions, I must find the ardent and the cautiously-decided. The ardent will advance and lay hold of truth; the cautiously-decided will keep themselves from what is wrong."

The Master said, "The people of the south have a saying—'A man without constancy cannot be either a wizard or a doctor.' Good!

"Inconstant in his virtue, he will be visited with disgrace."

The Master said, "This arises simply from not attending to the prognostication."

The Master said, "The superior man is affable, but not adulatory; the mean man is adulatory, but not affable."

Tsze-kung asked, saying, "What do you say of a man who is loved by all the people of his neighborhood?" The Master replied, "We may not for that accord our approval of him." "And what do you say of him who is hated by all the people of his neighborhood?" The Master said, "We may not for that conclude that he is bad. It is better than either of these cases that the good in the neighborhood love him, and the bad hate him."

The Master said, "The superior man is easy to serve and difficult to please. If you try to please him in any way which is not accordant with right, he will not be pleased. But in his employment of men, he uses them according to their capacity. The mean man is difficult to serve, and easy to please. If you try to please him, though it be in a way which is not accordant with right, he may be pleased. But in his employment of men, he wishes them to be equal to everything."

The Master said, "The superior man has a dignified ease without pride. The mean man has pride without a dignified ease."

The Master said, "The firm, the enduring, the simple, and the modest are near to virtue."

Tsze-lu asked, saying, "What qualities must a man possess to entitle him to be called a scholar?" The Master said, "He must be thus—earnest, urgent, and bland—among his friends, earnest and urgent; among his brethren, bland."

The Master said, "Let a good man teach the people seven years, and they may then likewise be employed in war."

The Master said, "To lead an uninstructed people to war, is to throw them away."

14

HSIEN ASKED what was shameful. The Master said, "When good government prevails in a state, to be thinking only of salary; and, when bad government prevails, to be thinking, in the same way, only of salary—this is shameful."

"When the love of superiority, boasting, resentments, and covetousness are repressed, this may be deemed perfect virtue."

The Master said, "This may be regarded as the achievement of what is difficult. But I do not know that it is to be deemed perfect virtue."

The Master said, "The scholar who cherishes the love of comfort is not fit to be deemed a scholar."

The Master said, "When good government prevails in a state, language may be lofty and bold, and actions the same. When bad government prevails, the actions may be lofty and bold, but the language may be with some reserve."

The Master said, "The virtuous will be sure to speak correctly, but those whose speech is good may not always be virtuous. Men of principle are sure to be bold, but those who are bold may not always be men of principle."

Nan-kung Kwo, submitting an inquiry to Confucius, said, "I was skillful at archery, and Ao could move a boat along upon the land, but neither of them died a natural death. Yu and Chi personally wrought at the toils of husbandry, and they became possessors of the kingdom." The Master made no reply; but when Nan-kung Kwo went out, he said, "A superior man indeed is this! An esteemer of virtue indeed is this!"

The Master said, "Superior men, and yet not always virtuous, there have been, alas! But there never has been a mean man, and, at the same time, virtuous."

The Master said, "Can there be love which does not lead to strictness with its object? Can there be loyalty which does not lead to the instruction of its object?"

The Master said, "In preparing the governmental notifications, P'i Shan first made the rough draft; Shi-shu examined and discussed its contents; Tsze-yu, the manager of foreign intercourse, then polished the style; and, finally, Tsze-ch'an of Tung-li gave it the proper elegance and finish."

Some one asked about Tsze-ch'an. The Master said, "He was a kind man."

He asked about Tsze-hsi. The Master said, "That man! That man!"

He asked about Kwan Chung. "For him," said the Master, "the city of Pien, with three hundred families, was taken from the chief of the Po family, who did not utter a murmuring word, though, to the end of his life, he had only coarse rice to eat."

The Master said, "To be poor without murmuring is difficult. To be rich without being proud is easy."

The Master said, "Mang Kung-ch'o is more than fit to be chief officer in the families of Chao and Wei, but he is not fit to be great officer to either of the states Tang or Hsieh."

Tsze-lu asked what constituted a COMPLETE man. The Master said, "Suppose a man with the knowledge of Tsang Wu-chung, the freedom from covetousness of Kung-ch'o, the bravery of Chwang of Pien, and the varied talents of Zan Ch'iu; add to these the accomplishments of the rules of propriety and music—such a one might be reckoned a COMPLETE man."

He then added, "But what is the necessity for a complete man of the present day to have all these things? The man, who in the view of gain, thinks of righteousness; who in the view of danger is prepared to give up his life; and who does not forget an old agreement however far back it extends—such a man may be reckoned a COMPLETE man."

The Master asked Kung-ming Chia about Kung-shu Wan, saying, "Is it true that your master speaks not, laughs not, and takes not?"

Kung-ming Chia replied, "This has arisen from the reporters going beyond the truth.—My master speaks when it is the time to speak, and so men do not get tired of his speaking. He laughs when there is occasion to be joyful, and so men do not get tired of his laughing. He takes when it is consistent with righteousness to do so, and so men do not get tired of his taking." The Master said, "So! But is it so with him?"

The Master said, "Tsang Wu-chung, keeping possession of Fang, asked of the duke of Lu to appoint a successor to him in his family. Although it may be said that he was not using force with his sovereign, I believe he was."

The Master said, "The duke Wan of Tsin was crafty and not upright. The duke Hwan of Ch'i was upright and not crafty."

Tsze-lu said, "The Duke Hwan caused his brother Chiu to be killed, when Shao Hu died, with his master, but Kwan Chung did not die. May not I say that he was wanting in virtue?"

The Master said, "The Duke Hwan assembled all the princes together, and that not with weapons of war and chariots—it was all through the influence of Kwan Chung. Whose beneficence was like his? Whose beneficence was like his?"

Tsze-kung said, "Kwan Chung, I apprehend was wanting in virtue. When the Duke Hwan caused his brother Chiu to be killed, Kwan Chung was not able to die with him. Moreover, he became prime minister to Hwan."

The Master said, "Kwan Chung acted as prime minister to the Duke Hwan made him leader of all the princes, and united and rectified the whole kingdom. Down to the present day, the people enjoy the gifts which he conferred. But for Kwan Chung, we should now be wearing our hair unbound, and the lappets of our coats buttoning on the left side.

"Will you require from him the small fidelity of common men and common women, who would commit suicide in a stream or ditch, no one knowing anything about them?"

The great officer, Hsien, who had been family minister to Kung-shu Wan, ascended to the prince's court in company with Wan.

The Master, having heard of it, said, "He deserved to be considered WAN (the accomplished)."

The Master was speaking about the unprincipled course of the duke Ling of Weil when Ch'i K'ang said, "Since he is of such a character, how is it he does not lose his state?"

Confucius said, "The Chung-shu Yu has the superintendence of his guests and of strangers; the litanist, T'o, has the management of his ancestral temple; and Wang-sun Chia has the direction of the army and forces—with such officers as these, how should he lose his state?"

The Master said, "He who speaks without modesty will find it difficult to make his words good."

Chan Ch'ang murdered the Duke Chien of Ch'i.

Confucius bathed, went to court and informed the Duke Ai, saying, "Chan Hang has slain his sovereign. I beg that you will undertake to punish him."

The duke said, "Inform the chiefs of the three families of it."

Confucius retired, and said, "Following in the rear of the great officers, I did not dare not to represent such a matter, and my prince says, 'Inform the chiefs of the three families of it.'"

He went to the chiefs, and informed them, but they would not act. Confucius then said, "Following in the rear of the great officers, I did not dare not to represent such a matter."

Tsze-lu asked how a ruler should be served. The Master said, "Do not impose on him, and, moreover, withstand him to his face."

The Master said, "The progress of the superior man is upwards; the progress of the mean man is downwards."

The Master said, "In ancient times, men learned with a view to their own improvement. Nowadays, men learn with a view to the approbation of others."

Chu Po-yu sent a messenger with friendly inquiries to Confucius.

Confucius sat with him, and questioned him. "What," said he, "is your master engaged in?" The messenger replied, "My master is anxious to make his faults few, but he has not yet succeeded." He then went out, and the Master said, "A messenger indeed! A messenger indeed!"

47

The Master said, "He who is not in any particular office has nothing to do with plans for the administration of its duties."

The philosopher Tsang said, "The superior man, in his thoughts, does not go out of his place."

The Master said, "The superior man is modest in his speech, but exceeds in his actions."

The Master said, "The way of the superior man is threefold, but I am not equal to it. Virtuous, he is free from anxieties; wise, he is free from perplexities; bold, he is free from fear."

Tsze-kung said, "Master, that is what you yourself say."

Tsze-kung was in the habit of comparing men together. The Master said, "Tsze must have reached a high pitch of excellence! Now, I have not leisure for this."

The Master said, "I will not be concerned at men's not knowing me; I will be concerned at my own want of ability."

The Master said, "He who does not anticipate attempts to deceive him, nor think beforehand of his not being believed, and yet apprehends these things readily when they occur—is he not a man of superior worth?"

Wei-shang Mau said to Confucius, "Ch'iu, how is it that you keep roosting about? Is it not that you are an insinuating talker?"

Confucius said, "I do not dare to play the part of such a talker, but I hate obstinacy."

The Master said, "A horse is called a ch'i, not because of its strength, but because of its other good qualities."

Some one said, "What do you say concerning the principle that injury should be recompensed with kindness?"

The Master said, "With what then will you recompense kindness?"

"Recompense injury with justice, and recompense kindness with kindness."

The Master said, "Alas! there is no one that knows me."

Tsze-kung said, "What do you mean by thus saying—that no one knows you?" The Master replied, "I do not murmur against Heaven. I do not grumble against men. My studies lie low, and my penetration rises high. But there is Heaven—that knows me!"

The Kung-po Liao, having slandered Tsze-lu to Chi-sun, Tsze-fu Ching-po informed Confucius of it, saying, "Our master is certainly being led astray by the Kung-po Liao, but I have still power enough left to cut Liao off, and expose his corpse in the market and in the court."

The Master said, "If my principles are to advance, it is so ordered. If they are to fall to the ground, it is so ordered. What can the Kung-po Liao do where such ordering is concerned?"

The Master said, "Some men of worth retire from the world. Some retire from particular states. Some retire because of disrespectful looks. Some retire because of contradictory language."

The Master said, "Those who have done this are seven men."

Tsze-lu happening to pass the night in Shih-man, the gatekeeper said to him, "Whom do you come from?" Tsze-lu said, "From Mr. K'ung." "It is he—is it not?" said the other, "who knows the impracticable nature of the times and yet will be doing in them."

The Master was playing, one day, on a musical stone in Weil when a man carrying a straw basket passed the door of the house where Confucius was, and said, "His heart is full who so beats the musical stone."

A little while after, he added, "How contemptible is the one-ideaed obstinacy those sounds display! When one is taken no notice of, he has simply at once to give over his wish for public employment. 'Deep water must be crossed with the clothes on; shallow water may be crossed with the clothes held up.'"

The Master said, "How determined is he in his purpose! But this is not difficult!"

Tsze-chang said, "What is meant when the Shu says that Kao-tsung, while observing the usual imperial mourning, was for three years without speaking?"

The Master said, "Why must Kao-tsung be referred to as an example of this? The ancients all did so. When the sovereign died, the officers all attended to their several duties, taking instructions from the prime minister for three years."

The Master said, "When rulers love to observe the rules of propriety, the people respond readily to the calls on them for service."

Tsze-lu asked what constituted the superior man. The Master said, "The cultivation of himself in reverential carefulness." "And is this all?" said Tsze-lu. "He cultivates himself so as to give rest to others," was the reply. "And is this all?" again asked Tsze-lu. The Master said, "He cultivates himself so as to give rest to all the people. He cultivates himself so as to give rest to all the people—even Yao and Shun were still solicitous about this."

Yuan Zang was squatting on his heels, and so waited the approach of the Master, who said to him, "In youth not humble as befits a junior; in manhood, doing nothing worthy of being handed down; and living on to old age—this is to be a pest." With this he hit him on the shank with his staff.

A youth of the village of Ch'ueh was employed by Confucius to carry the messages between him and his visitors. Some one asked about him, saying, "I suppose he has made great progress."

The Master said, "I observe that he is fond of occupying the seat of a full-grown man; I observe that he walks shoulder to shoulder with his elders. He is not one who is seeking to make progress in learning. He wishes quickly to become a man."

15

THE DUKE Ling of Wei asked Confucius about tactics. Confucius replied, "I have heard all about sacrificial vessels, but I have not learned military matters." On this, he took his departure the next day.

When he was in Chan, their provisions were exhausted, and his followers became so in that they were unable to rise.

Tsze-lu, with evident dissatisfaction, said, "Has the superior man likewise to endure in this way?" The Master said, "The superior man may indeed have to endure want, but the mean man, when he is in want, gives way to unbridled license."

The Master said, "Ts'ze, you think, I suppose, that I am one who learns many things and keeps them in memory?"

Tsze-kung replied, "Yes—but perhaps it is not so?"

"No," was the answer; "I seek a unity all pervading."

The Master said, "Yu I those who know virtue are few."

The Master said, "May not Shun be instanced as having governed efficiently without exertion? What did he do? He did nothing but gravely and reverently occupy his royal seat."

Tsze-chang asked how a man should conduct himself, so as to be everywhere appreciated.

The Master said, "Let his words be sincere and truthful and his actions honorable and careful—such conduct may be practiced among the rude tribes of the South or the North. If his words be not sincere and truthful and his actions not honorable and careful will he, with such conduct, be appreciated, even in his neighborhood?

"When he is standing, let him see those two things, as it were, fronting him. When he is in a carriage, let him see them attached to the yoke. Then may he subsequently carry them into practice."

Tsze-chang wrote these counsels on the end of his sash.

The Master said, "Truly straightforward was the historiographer Yu. When good government prevailed in his state, he was like an arrow. When bad government prevailed, he was like an arrow. A superior man indeed is Chu Po-yu! When good government prevails in his state, he is to be found in office. When bad government prevails, he can roll his principles up, and keep them in his breast."

The Master said, "When a man may be spoken with, not to speak to him is to err in reference to the man. When a man may not be spoken with, to speak to him is to err in reference to our words. The wise err neither in regard to their man nor to their words."

The Master said, "The determined scholar and the man of virtue will not seek to live at the expense of injuring their virtue. They will even sacrifice their lives to preserve their virtue complete."

Tsze-kung asked about the practice of virtue. The Master said, "The mechanic, who wishes to do his work well, must first sharpen his tools. When you are living in any state, take service with the most worthy among its great officers, and make friends of the most virtuous among its scholars."

Yen Yuan asked how the government of a country should be administered.

The Master said, "Follow the seasons of Hsia.

"Ride in the state carriage of Yin.

"Wear the ceremonial cap of Chau.

"Let the music be the Shao with its pantomimes. Banish the songs of Chang, and keep far from specious talkers. The songs of Chang are licentious; specious talkers are dangerous."

The Master said, "If a man take no thought about what is distant, he will find sorrow near at hand."

The Master said, "It is all over! I have not seen one who loves virtue as he loves beauty."

The Master said, "Was not Tsang Wan like one who had stolen his situation? He knew the virtue and the talents of Hui of Liu-hsia, and yet did not procure that he should stand with him in court."

The Master said, "He who requires much from himself and little from others, will keep himself from being the object of resentment."

The Master said, "When a man is not in the habit of saying—'What shall I think of this? What shall I think of this?' I can indeed do nothing with him!"

The Master said, "When a number of people are together, for a whole day, without their conversation turning on righteousness, and when they are fond of carrying out the suggestions of a small shrewdness—theirs is indeed a hard case."

The Master said, "The superior man in everything considers righteousness to be essential. He performs it according to the rules of propriety. He brings it forth in humility. He completes it with sincerity. This is indeed a superior man."

The Master said, "The superior man is distressed by his want of ability. He is not distressed by men's not knowing him."

The Master said, "The superior man dislikes the thought of his name not being mentioned after his death."

The Master said, "What the superior man seeks, is in himself. What the mean man seeks, is in others."

The Master said, "The superior man is dignified, but does not wrangle. He is sociable, but not a partisan."

The Master said, "The superior man does not promote a man simply on account of his words, nor does he put aside good words because of the man."

Tsze-kung asked, saying, "Is there one word which may serve as a rule of practice for all one's life?" The Master said, "Is not RECIPROCITY such a word? What you do not want done to yourself, do not do to others."

The Master said, "In my dealings with men, whose evil do I blame, whose goodness do I praise, beyond what is proper? If I do sometimes exceed in praise, there must be ground for it in my examination of the individual.

"This people supplied the ground why the three dynasties pursued the path of straightforwardness."

The Master said, "Even in my early days, a historiographer would leave a blank in his text, and he who had a horse would lend him to another to ride. Now, alas! there are no such things."

The Master said, "Specious words confound virtue. Want of forbearance in small matters confounds great plans."

The Master said, "When the multitude hate a man, it is necessary to examine into the case. When the multitude like a man, it is necessary to examine into the case."

The Master said, "A man can enlarge the principles which he follows; those principles do not enlarge the man."

The Master said, "To have faults and not to reform them—this, indeed, should be pronounced having faults."

The Master said, "I have been the whole day without eating, and the whole night without sleeping—occupied with thinking. It was of no use. The better plan is to learn."

The Master said, "The object of the superior man is truth. Food is not his object. There is plowing—even in that there is sometimes want. So with learning—emolument may be found in it. The superior man is anxious lest he should not get truth; he is not anxious lest poverty should come upon him."

The Master said, "When a man's knowledge is sufficient to attain, and his virtue is not sufficient to enable him to hold, whatever he may have gained, he will lose again.

"When his knowledge is sufficient to attain, and he has virtue enough to hold fast, if he cannot govern with dignity, the people will not respect him.

"When his knowledge is sufficient to attain, and he has virtue enough to hold fast; when he governs also with dignity, yet if he try to move the people contrary to the rules of propriety—full excellence is not reached."

The Master said, "The superior man cannot be known in little matters; but he may be intrusted with great concerns. The small man may not be intrusted with great concerns, but he may be known in little matters."

The Master said, "Virtue is more to man than either water or fire. I have seen men die from treading on water and fire, but I have never seen a man die from treading the course of virtue."

The Master said, "Let every man consider virtue as what devolves on himself. He may not yield the performance of it even to his teacher."

The Master said, "The superior man is correctly firm, and not firm merely."

The Master said, "A minister, in serving his prince, reverently discharges his duties, and makes his emolument a secondary consideration."

The Master said, "In teaching there should be no distinction of classes."

The Master said, "Those whose courses are different cannot lay plans for one another."

The Master said, "In language it is simply required that it convey the meaning."

The music master, Mien, having called upon him, when they came to the steps, the Master said, "Here are the steps." When they came to the mat for the guest to sit upon, he said, "Here is the mat." When all were seated, the Master informed him, saying, "So and so is here; so and so is here."

The music master, Mien, having gone out, Tsze-chang asked, saying, "Is it the rule to tell those things to the music master?"

The Master said, "Yes. This is certainly the rule for those who lead the blind."

16

THE HEAD of the Chi family was going to attack Chwan-yu.

Zan Yu and Chi-lu had an interview with Confucius, and said, "Our chief, Chil is going to commence operations against Chwan-yu."

Confucius said, "Ch'iu, is it not you who are in fault here?

"Now, in regard to Chwan-yu, long ago, a former king appointed its ruler to preside over the sacrifices to the eastern Mang; moreover, it is in the midst of the territory of our state; and its ruler is a minister in direct connection with the sovereign: What has your chief to do with attacking it?"

Zan Yu said, "Our master wishes the thing; neither of us two ministers wishes it."

Confucius said, "Ch'iu, there are the words of Chau Zan—'When he can put forth his ability, he takes his place in the ranks of office; when he finds himself unable to do so, he retires from it. How can he be used as a guide to a blind man, who does not support him when tottering, nor raise him up when fallen?'

"And further, you speak wrongly. When a tiger or rhinoceros escapes from his cage; when a tortoise or piece of jade is injured in its repository—whose is the fault?"

Zan Yu said, "But at present, Chwan-yu is strong and near to Pi; if our chief do not now take it, it will hereafter be a sorrow to his descendants."

Confucius said. "Ch'iu, the superior man hates those declining to say—'I want such and such a thing,' and framing explanations for their conduct.

"I have heard that rulers of states and chiefs of families are not troubled lest their people should be few, but are troubled lest they should not keep their several places; that they are not troubled with fears of poverty, but are troubled with fears of a want of contented repose among the people in their several places. For when the people keep their several places, there will be no poverty; when harmony prevails, there will be no scarcity of people; and when there is such a contented repose, there will be no rebellious upsettings.

"So it is.—Therefore, if remoter people are not submissive, all the influences of civil culture and virtue are to be cultivated to attract them to be so; and when they have been so attracted, they must be made contented and tranquil.

"Now, here are you, Yu and Ch'iu, assisting your chief. Remoter people are not submissive, and, with your help, he cannot attract them to him. In his own territory there are divisions and downfalls, leavings and separations, and, with your help, he cannot preserve it.

"And yet he is planning these hostile movements within the state.— I am afraid that the sorrow of the Chi-sun family will not be on account of Chwan-yu, but will be found within the screen of their own court."

Confucius said, "When good government prevails in the empire, ceremonies, music, and punitive military expeditions proceed from the son of Heaven. When bad government prevails in the empire, ceremonies, music, and punitive military expeditions proceed from the princes. When these things proceed from the princes, as a rule, the cases will be few in which they do not lose their power in ten generations. When they proceed from the great officers of the princes, as a rule, the case will be few in which they do not lose their power in five generations. When the subsidiary ministers of the great officers hold in their grasp the orders of the state, as a rule the cases will be few in which they do not lose their power in three generations.

"When right principles prevail in the kingdom, government will not be in the hands of the great officers.

"When right principles prevail in the kingdom, there will be no discussions among the common people."

Confucius said, "The revenue of the state has left the ducal house now for five generations. The government has been in the hands of the great officers for four generations. On this account, the descendants of the three Hwan are much reduced."

Confucius said, "There are three friendships which are advantageous, and three which are injurious. Friendship with the uplight; friendship with the sincere; and friendship with the man of much observation—these are advantageous. Friendship with the man of specious airs; friendship with the insinuatingly soft; and friendship with the glib-tongued—these are injurious."

Confucius said, "There are three things men find enjoyment in which are advantageous, and three things they find enjoyment in which are injurious. To find enjoyment in the discriminating study of ceremonies and music; to find enjoyment in speaking of the goodness of others; to find enjoyment in having many worthy friends—these are advantageous. To find enjoyment in extravagant pleasures; to find enjoyment in idleness and sauntering; to find enjoyment in the pleasures of feasting—these are injurious."

Confucius said, "There are three errors to which they who stand in the presence of a man of virtue and station are liable. They may speak when it does not come to them to speak—this is called rashness. They may not speak when it comes to them to speak—this is called concealment. They may speak without looking at the countenance of their superior—this is called blindness."

Confucius said, "There are three things which the superior man guards against. In youth, when the physical powers are not yet settled, he guards against lust. When he is strong and the physical powers are full of vigor, he guards against quarrelsomeness. When he is old, and the animal powers are decayed, he guards against covetousness."

Confucius said, "There are three things of which the superior man stands in awe. He stands in awe of the ordinances of Heaven. He stands in awe of great men. He stands in awe of the words of sages.

"The mean man does not know the ordinances of Heaven, and consequently does not stand in awe of them. He is disrespectful to great men. He makes sport of the words of sages."

Confucius said, "Those who are born with the possession of knowledge are the highest class of men. Those who learn, and so readily get possession of knowledge, are the next. Those who are dull and stupid, and yet compass the learning, are another class next to these. As to those who are dull and stupid and yet do not learn—they are the lowest of the people."

Confucius said, "The superior man has nine things which are subjects with him of thoughtful consideration. In regard to the use of his eyes, he is anxious to see clearly. In regard to the use of his ears, he is anxious to hear distinctly. In regard to his countenance, he is anxious that it should be benign. In regard to his demeanor, he is anxious that it should be respectful. In regard to his speech, he is anxious that it should be sincere. In regard to his doing of business, he is anxious that it should be reverently careful. In regard to what he doubts about, he is anxious to question others. When he is angry, he thinks of the difficulties his anger may involve him in. When he sees gain to be got, he thinks of righteousness."

Confucius said, "Contemplating good, and pursuing it, as if they could not reach it; contemplating evil! and shrinking from it, as they would from thrusting the hand into boiling water—I have seen such men, as I have heard such words.

"Living in retirement to study their aims, and practicing righteousness to carry out their principles—I have heard these words, but I have not seen such men."

The Duke Ching of Ch'i had a thousand teams, each of four horses, but on the day of his death, the people did not praise him for a single virtue. Po-i and Shu-ch'i died of hunger at the foot of the Shau-yang mountains, and the people, down to the present time, praise them.

"Is not that saying illustrated by this?"

Ch'an K'ang asked Po-yu, saying, "Have you heard any lessons from your father different from what we have all heard?"

Po-yu replied, "No. He was standing alone once, when I passed below the hall with hasty steps, and said to me, 'Have you learned the Odes?' On my replying 'Not yet,' he added, 'If you do not learn the Odes, you will not be fit to converse with.' I retired and studied the Odes.

"Another day, he was in the same way standing alone, when I passed by below the hall with hasty steps, and said to me, 'Have you learned the rules of Propriety?' On my replying 'Not yet,' he added, 'If you do not learn the rules of Propriety, your character cannot be established.' I then retired, and learned the rules of Propriety.

"I have heard only these two things from him."

Ch'ang K'ang retired, and, quite delighted, said, "I asked one thing, and I have got three things. I have heard about the Odes. I have heard about the rules of Propriety. I have also heard that the superior man maintains a distant reserve towards his son."

The wife of the prince of a state is called by him Fu Zan. She calls herself Hsiao T'ung. The people of the state call her Chun Fu Zan, and, to the people of other states, they call her K'wa Hsiao Chun. The people of other states also call her Chun Fu Zan.

17

YANG HO wished to see Confucius, but Confucius would not go to see him. On this, he sent a present of a pig to Confucius, who, having chosen a time when Ho was not at home went to pay his respects for the gift. He met him, however, on the way.

Ho said to Confucius, "Come, let me speak with you." He then asked, "Can he be called benevolent who keeps his jewel in his bosom, and leaves his country to confusion?" Confucius replied, "No." "Can he be called wise, who is anxious to be engaged in public employment, and yet is constantly losing the opportunity of being so?" Confucius again said, "No." "The days and months are passing away; the years do not wait for us." Confucius said, "Right; I will go into office."

The Master said, "By nature, men are nearly alike; by practice, they get to be wide apart."

The Master said, "There are only the wise of the highest class, and the stupid of the lowest class, who cannot be changed."

The Master, having come to Wu-ch'ang, heard there the sound of stringed instruments and singing.

Well pleased and smiling, he said, "Why use an ox knife to kill a fowl?"

Tsze-yu replied, "Formerly, Master, I heard you say—'When the man of high station is well instructed, he loves men; when the man of low station is well instructed, he is easily ruled.'"

The Master said, "My disciples, Yen's words are right. What I said was only in sport."

Kung-shan Fu-zao, when he was holding Pi, and in an attitude of rebellion, invited the Master to visit him, who was rather inclined to go.

Tsze-lu was displeased. and said, "Indeed, you cannot go! Why must you think of going to see Kung-shan?"

The Master said, "Can it be without some reason that he has invited ME? If any one employ me, may I not make an eastern Chau?"

Tsze-chang asked Confucius about perfect virtue. Confucius said, "To be able to practice five things everywhere under heaven constitutes perfect virtue." He begged to ask what they were, and was told, "Gravity, generosity of soul, sincerity, earnestness, and kindness. If you are grave, you will not be treated with disrespect. If you are generous, you will win all. If you are sincere, people will repose trust in you. If you are earnest, you will accomplish much. If you are kind, this will enable you to employ the services of others."

Pi Hsi inviting him to visit him, the Master was inclined to go.

Tsze-lu said, "Master, formerly I have heard you say, 'When a man in his own person is guilty of doing evil, a superior man will not associate with him.' Pi Hsi is in rebellion, holding possession of Chung-mau; if you go to him, what shall be said?"

The Master said, "Yes, I did use these words. But is it not said, that, if a thing be really hard, it may be ground without being made thin? Is it not said, that, if a thing be really white, it may be steeped in a dark fluid without being made black?

"Am I a bitter gourd? How can I be hung up out of the way of being eaten?"

The Master said, "Yu, have you heard the six words to which are attached six becloudings?" Yu replied, "I have not."

"Sit down, and I will tell them to you.

"There is the love of being benevolent without the love of learning—the beclouding here leads to a foolish simplicity. There is the love of knowing without the love of learning—the beclouding here leads to dissipation of mind. There is the love of being sincere without the love of learning—the beclouding here leads to an injurious disregard of consequences. There is the love of straightforwardness without the love of learning—the beclouding here leads to rudeness. There is the love of boldness without the love of learning—the beclouding here leads to insubordination. There is the love of firmness without the love of learning—the beclouding here leads to extravagant conduct."

The Master said, "My children, why do you not study the Book of Poetry?

"The Odes serve to stimulate the mind.

"They may be used for purposes of self-contemplation.

"They teach the art of sociability.

"They show how to regulate feelings of resentment.

"From them you learn the more immediate duty of serving one's father, and the remoter one of serving one's prince.

"From them we become largely acquainted with the names of birds, beasts, and plants."

The Master said to Po-yu, "Do you give yourself to the Chau-nan and the Shao-nan. The man who has not studied the Chau-nan and the Shao-nan is like one who stands with his face right against a wall. Is he not so?"

The Master said, "'It is according to the rules of propriety,' they say.—'It is according to the rules of propriety,' they say. Are gems and silk all that is meant by propriety? 'It is music,' they say.—'It is music,' they say. Are bells and drums all that is meant by music?"

The Master said, "He who puts on an appearance of stern firmness, while inwardly he is weak, is like one of the small, mean people—yea, is he not like the thief who breaks through, or climbs over, a wall?"

The Master said, "Your good, careful people of the villages are the thieves of virtue."

The Master said, "To tell, as we go along, what we have heard on the way, is to cast away our virtue."

The Master said, "There are those mean creatures! How impossible it is along with them to serve one's prince!

"While they have not got their aims, their anxiety is how to get them. When they have got them, their anxiety is lest they should lose them.

"When they are anxious lest such things should be lost, there is nothing to which they will not proceed."

The Master said, "Anciently, men had three failings, which now perhaps are not to be found.

"The high-mindedness of antiquity showed itself in a disregard of small things; the high-mindedness of the present day shows itself in wild license. The stern dignity of antiquity showed itself in grave reserve; the stern dignity of the present day shows itself in quarrelsome perverseness. The stupidity of antiquity showed itself in straight-forwardness; the stupidity of the present day shows itself in sheer deceit."

The Master said, "Fine words and an insinuating appearance are seldom associated with virtue."

The Master said, "I hate the manner in which purple takes away the luster of vermilion. I hate the way in which the songs of Chang confound the music of the Ya. I hate those who with their sharp mouths overthrow kingdoms and families."

The Master said, "I would prefer not speaking."

Tsze-kung said, "If you, Master, do not speak, what shall we, your disciples, have to record?"

The Master said, "Does Heaven speak? The four seasons pursue their courses, and all things are continually being produced, but does Heaven say anything?"

Zu Pei wished to see Confucius, but Confucius declined, on the ground of being sick, to see him. When the bearer of this message went out at the door, the Master took his lute and sang to it, in order that Pei might hear him.

Tsai Wo asked about the three years' mourning for parents, saying that one year was long enough.

"If the superior man," said he, "abstains for three years from the observances of propriety, those observances will be quite lost. If for three years he abstains from music, music will be ruined. Within a year the old grain is exhausted, and the new grain has sprung up, and, in procuring fire by friction, we go through all the changes of wood for that purpose. After a complete year, the mourning may stop."

The Master said, "If you were, after a year, to eat good rice, and wear embroidered clothes, would you feel at ease?" "I should," replied Wo.

The Master said, "If you can feel at ease, do it. But a superior man, during the whole period of mourning, does not enjoy pleasant food which he may eat, nor derive pleasure from music which he may hear. He also does not feel at ease, if he is comfortably lodged. Therefore he does not do what you propose. But now you feel at ease and may do it."

Tsai Wo then went out, and the Master said, "This shows Yu's want of virtue. It is not till a child is three years old that it is allowed to leave the arms of its parents. And the three years' mourning is universally observed throughout the empire. Did Yu enjoy the three years' love of his parents?"

The Master said, "Hard is it to deal with who will stuff himself with food the whole day, without applying his mind to anything good! Are there not gamesters and chess players? To be one of these would still be better than doing nothing at all."

Tsze-lu said, "Does the superior man esteem valor?" The Master said, "The superior man holds righteousness to be of highest importance. A man in a superior situation, having valor without righteousness, will be guilty of insubordination; one of the lower people having valor without righteousness, will commit robbery."

Tsze-kung said, "Has the superior man his hatreds also?" The Master said, "He has his hatreds. He hates those who proclaim the evil of others. He hates the man who, being in a low station, slanders his superiors. He hates those who have valor merely, and are unobservant of propriety. He hates those who are forward and determined, and, at the same time, of contracted understanding."

The Master then inquired, "Ts'ze, have you also your hatreds?" Tsze-kung replied, "I hate those who pry out matters, and ascribe the knowledge to their wisdom. I hate those who are only not modest, and think that they are valorous. I hate those who make known secrets, and think that they are straightforward."

The Master said, "Of all people, girls and servants are the most difficult to behave to. If you are familiar with them, they lose their humility. If you maintain a reserve towards them, they are discontented."

The Master said, "When a man at forty is the object of dislike, he will always continue what he is."

18

THE VISCOUNT of Wei withdrew from the court. The Viscount of Chi became a slave to Chau. Pi-kan remonstrated with him and died.

Confucius said, "The Yin dynasty possessed these three men of virtue."

Hui of Liu-hsia, being chief criminal judge, was thrice dismissed from his office. Some one said to him, "Is it not yet time for you, sir, to leave this?" He replied, "Serving men in an upright way, where shall I go to, and not experience such a thrice-repeated dismissal? If I choose to serve men in a crooked way, what necessity is there for me to leave the country of my parents?"

The duke Ching of Ch'i, with reference to the manner in which he should treat Confucius, said, "I cannot treat him as I would the chief of the Chi family. I will treat him in a manner between that accorded to the chief of the Chil and that given to the chief of the Mang family." He also said, "I am old; I cannot use his doctrines." Confucius took his departure.

The people of Ch'i sent to Lu a present of female musicians, which Chi Hwan received, and for three days no court was held. Confucius took his departure.

The madman of Ch'u, Chieh-yu, passed by Confucius, singing and saying, "O FANG! O FANG! How is your virtue degenerated! As to the past, reproof is useless; but the future may still be provided against. Give up your vain pursuit. Give up your vain pursuit. Peril awaits those who now engage in affairs of government."

Confucius alighted and wished to converse with him, but Chieh-yu hastened away, so that he could not talk with him.

Ch'ang-tsu and Chieh-ni were at work in the field together, when Confucius passed by them, and sent Tsze-lu to inquire for the ford.

Ch'ang-tsu said, "Who is he that holds the reins in the carriage there?" Tsze-lu told him, "It is K'ung Ch'iu." "Is it not K'ung of Lu?" asked he. "Yes," was the reply, to which the other rejoined, "He knows the ford."

Tsze-lu then inquired of Chieh-ni, who said to him, "Who are you, sir?" He answered, "I am Chung Yu." "Are you not the disciple of K'ung Ch'iu of Lu?" asked the other. "I am," replied he, and then Chieh-ni said to him, "Disorder, like a swelling flood, spreads over the whole empire, and who is he that will change its state for you? Rather than follow one who merely withdraws from this one and that one, had you not better follow those who have withdrawn from the world altogether?" With this he fell to covering up the seed, and proceeded with his work, without stopping.

Tsze-lu went and reported their remarks, when the Master observed with a sigh, "It is impossible to associate with birds and beasts, as if they were the same with us. If I associate not with these people—with mankind—with whom shall I associate? If right principles prevailed through the empire, there would be no use for me to change its state."

Tsze-lu, following the Master, happened to fall behind, when he met an old man, carrying across his shoulder on a staff a basket for weeds. Tsze-lu said to him, "Have you seen my master, sir?" The old man replied, "Your four limbs are unaccustomed to toil; you cannot distinguish the five kinds of grain—who is your master?" With this, he planted his staff in the ground, and proceeded to weed.

Tsze-lu joined his hands across his breast, and stood before him. The old man kept Tsze-lu to pass the night in his house, killed a fowl, prepared millet, and feasted him. He also introduced to him his two sons.

Next day, Tsze-lu went on his way, and reported his adventure. The Master said, "He is a recluse," and sent Tsze-lu back to see him again, but when he got to the place, the old man was gone.

Tsze-lu then said to the family, "Not to take office is not righteous. If the relations between old and young may not be neglected, how is it that he sets aside the duties that should be observed between sovereign and minister? Wishing to maintain his personal purity, he allows that great relation to come to confusion. A superior man takes office, and performs the righteous duties belonging to it. As to the failure of right principles to make progress, he is aware of that."

The men who have retired to privacy from the world have been Po-i, Shu-ch'i, Yuchung, I-yi, Chu-chang, Hui of Liu-hsia, and Shao-lien.

The Master said, "Refusing to surrender their wills, or to submit to any taint in their persons; such, I think, were Po-i and Shu-ch'i.

"It may be said of Hui of Liu-hsia! and of Shaolien, that they surrendered their wills, and submitted to taint in their persons, but their words corresponded with reason, and their actions were such as men are anxious to see. This is all that is to be remarked in them.

"It may be said of Yu-chung and I-yi, that, while they hid themselves in their seclusion, they gave a license to their words; but in their persons, they succeeded in preserving their purity, and, in their retirement, they acted according to the exigency of the times.

"I am different from all these. I have no course for which I am predetermined, and no course against which I am predetermined."

The grand music master, Chih, went to Ch'i.

Kan, the master of the band at the second meal, went to Ch'u. Liao, the band master at the third meal, went to Ts'ai. Chueh, the band master at the fourth meal, went to Ch'in.

Fang-shu, the drum master, withdrew to the north of the river.

Wu, the master of the hand drum, withdrew to the Han.

Yang, the assistant music master, and Hsiang, master of the musical stone, withdrew to an island in the sea.

The duke of Chau addressed his son, the duke of Lu, saying, "The virtuous prince does not neglect his relations. He does not cause the great ministers to repine at his not employing them. Without some great cause, he does not dismiss from their offices the members of old families. He does not seek in one man talents for every employment."

To Chau belonged the eight officers, Po-ta, Po-kwo, Chung-tu, Chung-hwu, Shu-ya, Shuhsia, Chi-sui, and Chi-kwa.

19

TSZE-CHANG said, "The scholar, trained for public duty, seeing threatening danger, is prepared to sacrifice his life. When the opportunity of gain is presented to him, he thinks of righteousness. In sacrificing, his thoughts are reverential. In mourning, his thoughts are about the grief which he should feel. Such a man commands our approbation indeed."

Tsze-chang said, "When a man holds fast to virtue, but without seeking to enlarge it, and believes in right principles, but without firm sincerity, what account can be made of his existence or non-existence?"

The disciples of Tsze-hsia asked Tsze-chang about the principles that should characterize mutual intercourse. Tsze-chang asked, "What does Tsze-hsia say on the subject?" They replied, "Tsze-hsia says: 'Associate with those who can advantage you. Put away from you those who cannot do so.'" Tsze-chang observed, "This is different from what I have learned. The superior man honors the talented and virtuous, and bears with all. He praises the good, and pities the incompetent. Am I possessed of great talents and virtue?—who is there among men whom I will not bear with? Am I devoid of talents and virtue?—men will put me away from them. What have we to do with the putting away of others?"

Tsze-hsia said, "Even in inferior studies and employments there is something worth being looked at; but if it be attempted to carry them out to what is remote, there is a danger of their proving inapplicable. Therefore, the superior man does not practice them."

Tsze-hsia said, "He, who from day to day recognizes what he has not yet, and from month to month does not forget what he has attained to, may be said indeed to love to learn."

Tsze-hsia said, "There are learning extensively, and having a firm and sincere aim; inquiring with earnestness, and reflecting with self-application—virtue is in such a course."

Tsze-hsia said, "Mechanics have their shops to dwell in, in order to accomplish their works. The superior man learns, in order to reach to the utmost of his principles."

Tsze-hsia said, "The mean man is sure to gloss his faults."

Tsze-hsia said, "The superior man undergoes three changes. Looked at from a distance, he appears stern; when approached, he is mild; when he is heard to speak, his language is firm and decided."

Tsze-hsia said, "The superior man, having obtained their confidence, may then impose labors on his people. If he have not gained their confidence, they will think that he is oppressing them. Having obtained the confidence of his prince, one may then remonstrate with him. If he have not gained his confidence, the prince will think that he is vilifying him."

Tsze-hsia said, "When a person does not transgress the boundary line in the great virtues, he may pass and repass it in the small virtues."

Tsze-yu said, "The disciples and followers of Tsze-hsia, in sprinkling and sweeping the ground, in answering and replying, in advancing and receding, are sufficiently accomplished. But these are only the branches of learning, and they are left ignorant of what is essential.— How can they be acknowledged as sufficiently taught?"

Tsze-hsia heard of the remark and said, "Alas! Yen Yu is wrong. According to the way of the superior man in teaching, what departments are there which he considers of prime importance, and delivers? what are there which he considers of secondary importance, and allows himself to be idle about? But as in the case of plants, which are assorted according to their classes, so he deals with his disciples. How can the way of a superior man be such as to make fools of any of them? Is it not the sage alone, who can unite in one the beginning and the consummation of learning?"

Tsze-hsia said, "The officer, having discharged all his duties, should devote his leisure to learning. The student, having completed his learning, should apply himself to be an officer."

Tsze-hsia said, "Mourning, having been carried to the utmost degree of grief, should stop with that."

Tsze-hsia said, "My friend Chang can do things which are hard to be done, but yet he is not perfectly virtuous."

The philosopher Tsang said, "How imposing is the manner of Chang! It is difficult along with him to practice virtue."

The philosopher Tsang said, "I heard this from our Master: 'Men may not have shown what is in them to the full extent, and yet they will be found to do so, on the occasion of mourning for their parents."

The philosopher Tsang said, "I have heard this from our Master— 'The filial piety of Mang Chwang, in other matters, was what other men are competent to, but, as seen in his not changing the ministers of his father, nor his father's mode of government, it is difficult to be attained to.'"

The chief of the Mang family having appointed Yang Fu to be chief criminal judge, the latter consulted the philosopher Tsang. Tsang said, "The rulers have failed in their duties, and the people consequently have been disorganized for a long time. When you have found out the truth of any accusation, be grieved for and pity them, and do not feel joy at your own ability."

Tsze-kung said, "Chau's wickedness was not so great as that name implies. Therefore, the superior man hates to dwell in a low-lying situation, where all the evil of the world will flow in upon him."

Tsze-kung said, "The faults of the superior man are like the eclipses of the sun and moon. He has his faults, and all men see them; he changes again, and all men look up to him."

Kung-sun Ch'ao of Wei asked Tszekung, saying, "From whom did Chung-ni get his learning?"

Tsze-kung replied, "The doctrines of Wan and Wu have not yet fallen to the ground. They are to be found among men. Men of talents and virtue remember the greater principles of them, and others, not possessing such talents and virtue, remember the smaller. Thus, all possess the doctrines of Wan and Wu. Where could our Master go that he should not have an opportunity of learning them? And yet what necessity was there for his having a regular master?"

Shu-sun Wu-shu observed to the great officers in the court, saying, "Tsze-kung is superior to Chung-ni."

Tsze-fu Ching-po reported the observation to Tsze-kung, who said, "Let me use the comparison of a house and its encompassing wall. My wall only reaches to the shoulders. One may peep over it, and see whatever is valuable in the apartments.

"The wall of my Master is several fathoms high. If one do not find the door and enter by it, he cannot see the ancestral temple with its beauties, nor all the officers in their rich array.

"But I may assume that they are few who find the door. Was not the observation of the chief only what might have been expected?"

Shu-sun Wu-shu having spoken revilingly of Chung-ni, Tsze-kung said, "It is of no use doing so. Chung-ni cannot be reviled. The talents and virtue of other men are hillocks and mounds which may be stepped over. Chung-ni is the sun or moon, which it is not possible to step over. Although a man may wish to cut himself off from the sage, what harm can he do to the sun or moon? He only shows that he does not know his own capacity."

Ch'an Tsze-ch'in, addressing Tsze-kung, said, "You are too modest. How can Chung-ni be said to be superior to you?"

Tsze-kung said to him, "For one word a man is often deemed to be wise, and for one word he is often deemed to be foolish. We ought to be careful indeed in what we say.

"Our Master cannot be attained to, just in the same way as the heavens cannot be gone up by the steps of a stair.

"Were our Master in the position of the ruler of a state or the chief of a family, we should find verified the description which has been given of a sage's rule—he would plant the people, and forthwith they would be established; he would lead them on, and forthwith they would follow him; he would make them happy, and forthwith multitudes would resort to his dominions; he would stimulate them, and forthwith they would be harmonious. While he lived, he would be glorious. When he died, he would be bitterly lamented. How is it possible for him to be attained to?"

20

YAO said, "Oh! you, Shun, the Heaven-determined order of succession now rests in your person. Sincerely hold fast the due Mean. If there shall be distress and want within the four seas, the Heavenly revenue will come to a perpetual end."

Shun also used the same language in giving charge to Yu.

T'ang said, "I the child Li, presume to use a dark-colored victim, and presume to announce to Thee, O most great and sovereign God, that the sinner I dare not pardon, and thy ministers, O God, I do not keep in obscurity. The examination of them is by thy mind, O God. If, in my person, I commit offenses, they are not to be attributed to you, the people of the myriad regions. If you in the myriad regions commit offenses, these offenses must rest on my person."

Chau conferred great gifts, and the good were enriched.

"Although he has his near relatives, they are not equal to my virtuous men. The people are throwing blame upon me, the One man."

He carefully attended to the weights and measures, examined the body of the laws, restored the discarded officers, and the good government of the kingdom took its course.

He revived states that had been extinguished, restored families whose line of succession had been broken, and called to office those who had retired into obscurity, so that throughout the kingdom the hearts of the people turned towards him.

What he attached chief importance to were the food of the people, the duties of mourning, and sacrifices.

By his generosity, he won all. By his sincerity, he made the people repose trust in him. By his earnest activity, his achievements were great. By his justice, all were delighted.

Tsze-chang asked Confucius, saying, "In what way should a person in authority act in order that he may conduct government properly?" The Master replied, "Let him honor the five excellent, and banish away the four bad, things—then may he conduct government properly." Tsze-chang said, "What are meant by the five excellent things?" The Master said, "When the person in authority is beneficent without great expenditure; when he lays tasks on the people without their repining; when he pursues what he desires without being covetous; when he maintains a dignified ease without being proud; when he is majestic without being fierce."

Tsze-chang said, "What is meant by being beneficent without great expenditure?" The Master replied, "When the person in authority makes more beneficial to the people the things from which they naturally derive benefit—is not this being beneficent without great expenditure? When he chooses the labors which are proper, and makes them labor on them, who will repine? When his desires are set on benevolent government, and he secures it, who will accuse him of covetousness? Whether he has to do with many people or few, or with things great or small, he does not dare to indicate any disrespect—is not this to maintain a dignified ease without any pride? He adjusts his clothes and cap, and throws a dignity into his looks, so that, thus dignified, he is looked at with awe—is not this to be majestic without being fierce?"

Tsze-chang then asked, "What are meant by the four bad things?" The Master said, "To put the people to death without having instructed them—this is called cruelty. To require from them, suddenly, the full tale of work, without having given them warning—this is called oppression. To issue orders as if without urgency, at first, and, when the time comes, to insist on them with severity—this is called injury. And, generally, in the giving pay or rewards to men, to do it in a stingy way—this is called acting the part of a mere official."

The Master said, "Without recognizing the ordinances of Heaven, it is impossible to be a superior man.

"Without an acquaintance with the rules of Propriety, it is impossible for the character to be established.

"Without knowing the force of words, it is impossible to know men."

THE DOCTRINE OF THE MEAN

WHAT HEAVEN has conferred is called The Nature; an accordance with this nature is called The Path of duty; the regulation of this path is called Instruction.

The path may not be left for an instant. If it could be left, it would not be the path. On this account, the superior man does not wait till he sees things, to be cautious, nor till he hears things, to be apprehensive.

There is nothing more visible than what is secret, and nothing more manifest than what is minute. Therefore the superior man is watchful over himself, when he is alone.

While there are no stirrings of pleasure, anger, sorrow, or joy, the mind may be said to be in the state of Equilibrium. When those feelings have been stirred, and they act in their due degree, there ensues what may be called the state of Harmony. This Equilibrium is the great root from which grow all the human actings in the world, and this Harmony is the universal path which they all should pursue.

Let the states of equilibrium and harmony exist in perfection, and a happy order will prevail throughout heaven and earth, and all things will be nourished and flourish.

Chung-ni said, "The superior man embodies the course of the Mean; the mean man acts contrary to the course of the Mean.

"The superior man's embodying the course of the Mean is because he is a superior man, and so always maintains the Mean. The mean man's acting contrary to the course of the Mean is because he is a mean man, and has no caution."

The Master said, "Perfect is the virtue which is according to the Mean! Rare have they long been among the people, who could practice it!"

The Master said, "I know how it is that the path of the Mean is not walked in—The knowing go beyond it, and the stupid do not come up to it. I know how it is that the path of the Mean is not understood— The men of talents and virtue go beyond it, and the worthless do not come up to it.

"There is no body but eats and drinks. But they are few who can distinguish flavors."

The Master said, "Alas! How is the path of the Mean untrodden!"

The Master said, "There was Shun—He indeed was greatly wise! Shun loved to question others, and to study their words, though they might be shallow. He concealed what was bad in them and displayed what was good. He took hold of their two extremes, determined the Mean, and employed it in his government of the people. It was by this that he was Shun!"

The Master said "Men all say, 'We are wise'; but being driven forward and taken in a net, a trap, or a pitfall, they know not how to escape. Men all say, 'We are wise'; but happening to choose the course of the Mean, they are not able to keep it for a round month."

The Master said, "This was the manner of Hui—he made choice of the Mean, and whenever he got hold of what was good, he clasped it firmly, as if wearing it on his breast, and did not lose it."

The Master said, "The kingdom, its states, and its families, may be perfectly ruled; dignities and emoluments may be declined; naked weapons may be trampled under the feet; but the course of the Mean cannot be attained to."

Tsze-lu asked about energy.

The Master said, "Do you mean the energy of the South, the energy of the North, or the energy which you should cultivate yourself?

"To show forbearance and gentleness in teaching others; and not to revenge unreasonable conduct—this is the energy of southern regions, and the good man makes it his study.

"To lie under arms; and meet death without regret—this is the energy of northern regions, and the forceful make it their study.

"Therefore, the superior man cultivates a friendly harmony, without being weak.—How firm is he in his energy! He stands erect in the middle, without inclining to either side.—How firm is he in his energy! When good principles prevail in the government of his country, he does not change from what he was in retirement. How firm is he in his energy! When bad principles prevail in the country, he maintains his course to death without changing.—How firm is he in his energy!"

The Master said, "To live in obscurity, and yet practice wonders, in order to be mentioned with honor in future ages—this is what I do not do.

"The good man tries to proceed according to the right path, but when he has gone halfway, he abandons it—I am not able so to stop.

"The superior man accords with the course of the Mean. Though he may be all unknown, unregarded by the world, he feels no regret.—It is only the sage who is able for this."

The way which the superior man pursues, reaches wide and far, and yet is secret.

Common men and women, however ignorant, may intermeddle with the knowledge of it; yet in its utmost reaches, there is that which even the sage does not know. Common men and women, however much below the ordinary standard of character, can carry it into practice; yet in its utmost reaches, there is that which even the sage is not able to carry into practice. Great as heaven and earth are, men still find some things in them with which to be dissatisfied. Thus it is that, were the superior man to speak of his way in all its greatness, nothing in the world would be found able to embrace it, and were he to speak of it in its minuteness, nothing in the world would be found able to split it.

It is said in the Book of Poetry, "The hawk flies up to heaven; the fishes leap in the deep." This expresses how this way is seen above and below.

The way of the superior man may be found, in its simple elements, in the intercourse of common men and women; but in its utmost reaches, it shines brightly through Heaven and earth.

The Master said, "The path is not far from man. When men try to pursue a course, which is far from the common indications of consciousness, this course cannot be considered The Path.

"In the Book of Poetry, it is said, 'In hewing an ax handle, in hewing an ax handle, the pattern is not far off. We grasp one ax handle to hew the other; and yet, if we look askance from the one to the other, we may consider them as apart. Therefore, the superior man governs men, according to their nature, with what is proper to them, and as soon as they change what is wrong, he stops.

"When one cultivates to the utmost the principles of his nature, and exercises them on the principle of reciprocity, he is not far from the path. What you do not like when done to yourself, do not do to others.

"In the way of the superior man there are four things, to not one of which have I as yet attained.—To serve my father, as I would require my son to serve me: to this I have not attained; to serve my prince as I would require my minister to serve me: to this I have not attained; to serve my elder brother as I would require my younger brother to serve me: to this I have not attained; to set the example in behaving to a friend, as I would require him to behave to me: to this I have not attained. Earnest in practicing the ordinary virtues, and careful in speaking about them, if, in his practice, he has anything defective, the superior man dares not but exert himself; and if, in his words, he has any excess, he dares not allow himself such license. Thus his words have respect to his actions, and his actions have respect to his words; is it not just an entire sincerity which marks the superior man?"

The superior man does what is proper to the station in which he is; he does not desire to go beyond this.

In a position of wealth and honor, he does what is proper to a position of wealth and honor. In a poor and low position, he does what is proper to a poor and low position. Situated among barbarous tribes, he does what is proper to a situation among barbarous tribes. In a position of sorrow and difficulty, he does what is proper to a position of sorrow and difficulty. The superior man can find himself in no situation in which he is not himself.

In a high situation, he does not treat with contempt his inferiors. In a low situation, he does not court the favor of his superiors. He rectifies himself, and seeks for nothing from others, so that he has no dissatisfactions. He does not murmur against Heaven, nor grumble against men.

Thus it is that the superior man is quiet and calm, waiting for the appointments of Heaven, while the mean man walks in dangerous paths, looking for lucky occurrences.

The Master said, "In archery we have something like the way of the superior man. When the archer misses the center of the target, he turns round and seeks for the cause of his failure in himself."

The way of the superior man may be compared to what takes place in traveling, when to go to a distance we must first traverse the space that is near, and in ascending a height, when we must begin from the lower ground.

It is said in the Book of Poetry, "Happy union with wife and children is like the music of lutes and harps. When there is concord among brethren, the harmony is delightful and enduring. Thus may you regulate your family, and enjoy the pleasure of your wife and children."

The Master said, "In such a state of things, parents have entire complacence!"

The Master said, "How abundantly do spiritual beings display the powers that belong to them!

"We look for them, but do not see them; we listen to, but do not hear them; yet they enter into all things, and there is nothing without them.

"They cause all the people in the kingdom to fast and purify themselves, and array themselves in their richest dresses, in order to attend at their sacrifices. Then, like overflowing water, they seem to be over the heads, and on the right and left of their worshippers.

"It is said in the Book of Poetry, 'The approaches of the spirits, you cannot sunrise; and can you treat them with indifference?'

"Such is the manifestness of what is minute! Such is the impossibility of repressing the outgoings of sincerity!"

The Master said, "How greatly filial was Shun! His virtue was that of a sage; his dignity was the throne; his riches were all within the four seas. He offered his sacrifices in his ancestral temple, and his descendants preserved the sacrifices to himself.

"Therefore having such great virtue, it could not but be that he should obtain the throne, that he should obtain those riches, that he should obtain his fame, that he should attain to his long life.

"Thus it is that Heaven, in the production of things, is sure to be bountiful to them, according to their qualities. Hence the tree that is flourishing, it nourishes, while that which is ready to fall, it overthrows.

"In the Book of Poetry, it is said, 'The admirable amiable prince displayed conspicuously his excelling virtue, adjusting his people, and adjusting his officers. Therefore, he received from Heaven his emoluments of dignity. It protected him, assisted him, decreed him the throne; sending from Heaven these favors, as it were repeatedly.'

"We may say therefore that he who is greatly virtuous will be sure to receive the appointment of Heaven."

The Master said, "It is only King Wan of whom it can be said that he had no cause for grief! His father was King Chi, and his son was King Wu. His father laid the foundations of his dignity, and his son transmitted it.

"King Wu continued the enterprise of King T'ai, King Chi, and King Wan. He once buckled on his armor, and got possession of the kingdom. He did not lose the distinguished personal reputation which he had throughout the kingdom. His dignity was the royal throne. His riches were the possession of all within the four seas. He offered his sacrifices in his ancestral temple, and his descendants maintained the sacrifices to himself.

"It was in his old age that King Wu received the appointment to the throne, and the duke of Chau completed the virtuous course of Wan and Wu. He carried up the title of king to T'ai and Chi, and sacrificed to all the former dukes above them with the royal ceremonies. And this rule he extended to the princes of the kingdom, the great officers, the scholars, and the common people. If the father were a great officer and the son a scholar, then the burial was that due to a great officer, and the sacrifice that due to a scholar. If the father were a scholar and the son a great officer, then the burial was that due to a scholar, and the sacrifice that due to a great officer. The one year's mourning was made to extend only to the great officers, but the three years' mourning extended to the Son of Heaven. In the mourning for a father or mother, he allowed no difference between the noble and the mean.

The Master said, "How far-extending was the filial piety of King Wu and the duke of Chau!

"Now filial piety is seen in the skillful carrying out of the wishes of our forefathers, and the skillful carrying forward of their undertakings.

"In spring and autumn, they repaired and beautified the temple halls of their fathers, set forth their ancestral vessels, displayed their various robes, and presented the offerings of the several seasons.

"By means of the ceremonies of the ancestral temple, they distinguished the royal kindred according to their order of descent. By ordering the parties present according to their rank, they distinguished the more noble and the less. By the arrangement of the services, they made a distinction of talents and worth. In the ceremony of general pledging, the inferiors presented the cup to their superiors, and thus something was given the lowest to do. At the concluding feast, places were given according to the hair, and thus was made the distinction of years.

"They occupied the places of their forefathers, practiced their ceremonies, and performed their music. They reverenced those whom they honored, and loved those whom they regarded with affection. Thus they served the dead as they would have served them alive; they served the departed as they would have served them had they been continued among them.

"By the ceremonies of the sacrifices to Heaven and Earth they served God, and by the ceremonies of the ancestral temple they sacrificed to their ancestors. He who understands the ceremonies of the sacrifices to Heaven and Earth, and the meaning of the several sacrifices to ancestors, would find the government of a kingdom as easy as to look into his palm!"

The Duke Ai asked about government.

The Master said, "The government of Wan and Wu is displayed in the records—the tablets of wood and bamboo. Let there be the men and the government will flourish; but without the men, their government decays and ceases.

"With the right men the growth of government is rapid, just as vegetation is rapid in the earth; and, moreover, their government might be called an easily-growing rush.

"Therefore the administration of government lies in getting proper men. Such men are to be got by means of the ruler's own character. That character is to be cultivated by his treading in the ways of duty. And the treading those ways of duty is to be cultivated by the cherishing of benevolence.

"Benevolence is the characteristic element of humanity, and the great exercise of it is in loving relatives. Righteousness is the accordance of actions with what is right, and the great exercise of it is in honoring the worthy. The decreasing measures of the love due to relatives, and the steps in the honor due to the worthy, are produced by the principle of propriety.

"When those in inferior situations do not possess the confidence of their superiors, they cannot retain the government of the people.

"Hence the sovereign may not neglect the cultivation of his own character. Wishing to cultivate his character, he may not neglect to serve his parents. In order to serve his parents, he may not neglect to acquire knowledge of men. In order to know men, he may not dispense with a knowledge of Heaven.

"The duties of universal obligation are five and the virtues wherewith they are practiced are three. The duties are those between sovereign and minister, between father and son, between husband and wife, between elder brother and younger, and those belonging to the intercourse of friends. Those five are the duties of universal obligation. Knowledge, magnanimity, and energy, these three, are the virtues universally binding. And the means by which they carry the duties into practice is singleness.

"Some are born with the knowledge of those duties; some know them by study; and some acquire the knowledge after a painful feeling of their ignorance. But the knowledge being possessed, it comes to the same thing. Some practice them with a natural ease; some from a desire for their advantages; and some by strenuous effort. But the achievement being made, it comes to the same thing."

The Master said, "To be fond of learning is to be near to knowledge. To practice with vigor is to be near to magnanimity. To possess the feeling of shame is to be near to energy.

"He who knows these three things knows how to cultivate his own character. Knowing how to cultivate his own character, he knows how to govern other men. Knowing how to govern other men, he knows how to govern the kingdom with all its states and families.

"All who have the government of the kingdom with its states and families have nine standard rules to follow—viz., the cultivation of their own characters; the honoring of men of virtue and talents; affection towards their relatives; respect towards the great ministers; kind and considerate treatment of the whole body of officers; dealing with the mass of the people as children; encouraging the resort of all classes of artisans; indulgent treatment of men from a distance; and the kindly cherishing of the princes of the states.

"By the ruler's cultivation of his own character, the duties of universal obligation are set forth. By honoring men of virtue and talents, he is preserved from errors of judgment. By showing affection to his relatives, there is no grumbling nor resentment among his uncles and brethren. By respecting the great ministers, he is kept from errors in the practice of government. By kind and considerate treatment of the whole body of officers, they are led to make the most grateful return for his courtesies. By dealing with the mass of the people as his children, they are led to exhort one another to what is good. By encouraging the resort of all classes of artisans, his resources for expenditure are rendered ample. By indulgent treatment of men from a distance, they are brought to resort to him from all quarters. And by kindly cherishing the princes of the states, the whole kingdom is brought to revere him.

"Self-adjustment and purification, with careful regulation of his dress, and then not making a movement contrary to the rules of propriety—this is the way for a ruler to cultivate his person. Discarding slanderers, and keeping himself from the seductions of beauty; making light of riches, and giving honor to virtue—this is the way for him to encourage men of worth and talents. Giving them places of honor and large emolument, and sharing with them in their likes and dislikes—this is the way for him to encourage his relatives to love him. Giving them numerous officers to discharge their orders and commissions—this is the way for him to encourage the great ministers. According to them a generous confidence, and making their emoluments large—this is the way to encourage the body of officers. Employing them only at the proper times, and making the imposts light—this is the way to encourage the people. By daily examinations and monthly trials, and by making their rations in accordance with their labors—this is the way to encourage the classes of artisans. To escort them on their departure and meet them on their coming; to commend the good among them, and show compassion to the incompetent—this is the way to treat indulgently men from a distance. To restore families whose line of succession has been broken, and to revive states that have been extinguished; to reduce to order states that are in confusion, and support those which are in peril; to have fixed times for their own reception at court, and the reception of their envoys; to send them away after liberal treatment, and welcome their coming with small contributions—this is the way to cherish the princes of the states.

"All who have the government of the kingdom with its states and families have the above nine standard rules. And the means by which they are carried into practice is singleness.

"In all things success depends on previous preparation, and without such previous preparation there is sure to be failure. If what is to be spoken be previously determined, there will be no stumbling. If affairs be previously determined, there will be no difficulty with them. If one's actions have been previously determined, there will be no sorrow in connection with them. If principles of conduct have been previously determined, the practice of them will be inexhaustible.

"When those in inferior situations do not obtain the confidence of the sovereign, they cannot succeed in governing the people. There is a way to obtain the confidence of the sovereign—if one is not trusted by his friends, he will not get the confidence of his sovereign. There is a way to being trusted by one's friends—if one is not obedient to his parents, he will not be true to friends. There is a way to being obedient to one's parents—if one, on turning his thoughts in upon himself, finds a want of sincerity, he will not be obedient to his parents. There is a way to the attainment of sincerity in one's self—if a man do not understand what is good, he will not attain sincerity in himself.

"Sincerity is the way of Heaven. The attainment of sincerity is the way of men. He who possesses sincerity is he who, without an effort, hits what is right, and apprehends, without the exercise of thought—he is the sage who naturally and easily embodies the right way. He who attains to sincerity is he who chooses what is good, and firmly holds it fast.

"To this attainment there are requisite the extensive study of what is good, accurate inquiry about it, careful reflection on it, the clear discrimination of it, and the earnest practice of it.

"The superior man, while there is anything he has not studied, or while in what he has studied there is anything he cannot understand, will not intermit his labor. While there is anything he has not inquired about, or anything in what he has inquired about which he does not know, he will not intermit his labor. While there is anything which he has not reflected on, or anything in what he has reflected on which he does not apprehend, he will not intermit his labor. While there is anything which he has not discriminated or his discrimination is not clear, he will not intermit his labor. If there be anything which he has not practiced, or his practice fails in earnestness, he will not intermit his labor. If another man succeed by one effort, he will use a hundred efforts. If another man succeed by ten efforts, he will use a thousand.

"Let a man proceed in this way, and, though dull, he will surely become intelligent; though weak, he will surely become strong."

When we have intelligence resulting from sincerity, this condition is to be ascribed to nature; when we have sincerity resulting from intelligence, this condition is to be ascribed to instruction. But given the sincerity, and there shall be the intelligence; given the intelligence, and there shall be the sincerity.

It is only he who is possessed of the most complete sincerity that can exist under heaven, who can give its fun development to his nature. Able to give its full development to his own nature, he can do the same to the nature of other men. Able to give its full development to the nature of other men, he can give their full development to the natures of animals and things. Able to give their full development to the natures of creatures and things, he can assist the transforming and nourishing powers of Heaven and Earth. Able to assist the transforming and nourishing powers of Heaven and Earth, he may with Heaven and Earth form a ternion.

Next to the above is he who cultivates to the utmost the shoots of goodness in him. From those he can attain to the possession of sincerity. This sincerity becomes apparent. From being apparent, it becomes manifest. From being manifest, it becomes brilliant. Brilliant, it affects others. Affecting others, they are changed by it. Changed by it, they are transformed. It is only he who is possessed of the most complete sincerity that can exist under heaven, who can transform.

It is characteristic of the most entire sincerity to be able to foreknow. When a nation or family is about to flourish, there are sure to be happy omens; and when it is about to perish, there are sure to be unlucky omens. Such events are seen in the milfoil and tortoise, and affect the movements of the four limbs. When calamity or happiness is about to come, the good shall certainly be foreknown by him, and the evil also. Therefore the individual possessed of the most complete sincerity is like a spirit.

Sincerity is that whereby self-completion is effected, and its way is that by which man must direct himself.

Sincerity is the end and beginning of things; without sincerity there would be nothing. On this account, the superior man regards the attainment of sincerity as the most excellent thing.

The possessor of sincerity does not merely accomplish the self-completion of himself. With this quality he completes other men and things also. The completing himself shows his perfect virtue. The completing other men and things shows his knowledge. But these are virtues belonging to the nature, and this is the way by which a union is effected of the external and internal. Therefore, whenever he—the entirely sincere man—employs them—that is, these virtues, their action will be right.

Hence to entire sincerity there belongs ceaselessness.

Not ceasing, it continues long. Continuing long, it evidences itself.

Evidencing itself, it reaches far. Reaching far, it becomes large and substantial. Large and substantial, it becomes high and brilliant.

Large and substantial—this is how it contains all things. High and brilliant—this is how it overspreads all things. Reaching far and continuing long—this is how it perfects all things.

So large and substantial, the individual possessing it is the co-equal of Earth. So high and brilliant, it makes him the co-equal of Heaven. So far-reaching and long-continuing, it makes him infinite.

Such being its nature, without any display, it becomes manifested; without any movement, it produces changes; and without any effort, it accomplishes its ends.

The way of Heaven and Earth may be completely declared in one sentence.—They are without any doubleness, and so they produce things in a manner that is unfathomable.

The way of Heaven and Earth is large and substantial, high and brilliant, far-reaching and long-enduring.

The Heaven now before us is only this bright shining spot; but when viewed in its inexhaustible extent, the sun, moon, stars, and constellations of the zodiac, are suspended in it, and all things are over-spread by it. The earth before us is but a handful of soil; but when regarded in its breadth and thickness, it sustains mountains like the Hwa and the Yo, without feeling their weight, and contains the rivers and seas, without their leaking away. The mountain now before us appears only a stone; but when contemplated in all the vastness of its size, we see how the grass and trees are produced on it, and birds and beasts dwell on it, and precious things which men treasure up are found on it. The water now before us appears but a ladleful; yet extending our view to its unfathomable depths, the largest tortoises, iguanas, iguanodons, dragons, fishes, and turtles, are produced in it, articles of value and sources of wealth abound in it.

It is said in the Book of Poetry, "The ordinances of Heaven, how profound are they and unceasing!" The meaning is, that it is thus that Heaven is Heaven. And again, "How illustrious was it, the singleness of the virtue of King Wan!" indicating that it was thus that King Wan was what he was. Singleness likewise is unceasing.

How great is the path proper to the Sage!

Like overflowing water, it sends forth and nourishes all things, and rises up to the height of heaven.

All-complete is its greatness! It embraces the three hundred rules of ceremony, and the three thousand rules of demeanor.

It waits for the proper man, and then it is trodden.

Hence it is said, "Only by perfect virtue can the perfect path, in all its courses, be made a fact."

Therefore, the superior man honors his virtuous nature, and maintains constant inquiry and study, seeking to carry it out to its breadth and greatness, so as to omit none of the more exquisite and minute points which it embraces, and to raise it to its greatest height and brilliancy, so as to pursue the course of the Mean. He cherishes his old knowledge, and is continually acquiring new. He exerts an honest, generous earnestness, in the esteem and practice of all propriety.

Thus, when occupying a high situation he is not proud, and in a low situation he is not insubordinate. When the kingdom is well governed, he is sure by his words to rise; and when it is ill governed, he is sure by his silence to command forbearance to himself. Is not this what we find in the Book of Poetry—"Intelligent is he and prudent, and so preserves his person?"

The Master said, "Let a man who is ignorant be fond of using his own judgment; let a man without rank be fond of assuming a directing power to himself; let a man who is living in the present age go back to the ways of antiquity—on the persons of all who act thus calamities will be sure to come."

To no one but the Son of Heaven does it belong to order ceremonies, to fix the measures, and to determine the written characters.

Now over the kingdom, carriages have all wheels, of the same size; all writing is with the same characters; and for conduct there are the same rules.

One may occupy the throne, but if he have not the proper virtue, he may not dare to make ceremonies or music. One may have the virtue, but if he do not occupy the throne, he may not presume to make ceremonies or music.

The Master said, "I may describe the ceremonies of the Hsia dynasty, but Chi cannot sufficiently attest my words. I have learned the ceremonies of the Yin dynasty, and in Sung they still continue. I have learned the ceremonies of Chau, which are now used, and I follow Chau."

He who attains to the sovereignty of the kingdom, having those three important things, shall be able to effect that there shall be few errors under his government.

However excellent may have been the regulations of those of former times, they cannot be attested. Not being attested, they cannot command credence, and not being credited, the people would not follow them. However excellent might be the regulations made by one in an inferior situation, he is not in a position to be honored. Unhonored, he cannot command credence, and not being credited, the people would not follow his rules.

Therefore the institutions of the Ruler are rooted in his own character and conduct, and sufficient attestation of them is given by the masses of the people. He examines them by comparison with those of the three kings, and finds them without mistake. He sets them up before Heaven and Earth, and finds nothing in them contrary to their mode of operation. He presents himself with them before spiritual beings, and no doubts about them arise. He is prepared to wait for the rise of a sage a hundred ages after, and has no misgivings.

His presenting himself with his institutions before spiritual beings, without any doubts arising about them, shows that he knows Heaven. His being prepared, without any misgivings, to wait for the rise of a sage a hundred ages after, shows that he knows men.

Such being the case, the movements of such a ruler, illustrating his institutions, constitute an example to the world for ages. His acts are for ages a law to the kingdom. His words are for ages a lesson to the kingdom. Those who are far from him look longingly for him; and those who are near him are never wearied with him.

It is said in the Book of Poetry, "Not disliked there, not tired of here, from day to day and night tonight, will they perpetuate their praise." Never has there been a ruler, who did not realize this description, that obtained an early renown throughout the kingdom.

Chung-ni handed down the doctrines of Yao and Shun, as if they had been his ancestors, and elegantly displayed the regulations of Wan and Wul taking them as his model. Above, he harmonized with the times of Heaven, and below, he was conformed to the water and land.

He may be compared to Heaven and Earth in their supporting and containing, their overshadowing and curtaining, all things. He may be compared to the four seasons in their alternating progress, and to the sun and moon in their successive shining.

All things are nourished together without their injuring one another. The courses of the seasons, and of the sun and moon, are pursued without any collision among them. The smaller energies are like river currents; the greater energies are seen in mighty transformations. It is this which makes heaven and earth so great.

It is only he, possessed of all sagely qualities that can exist under heaven, who shows himself quick in apprehension, clear in discernment, of far-reaching intelligence, and all-embracing knowledge, fitted to exercise rule; magnanimous, generous, benign, and mild, fitted to exercise forbearance; impulsive, energetic, firm, and enduring, fitted to maintain a firm hold; self-adjusted, grave, never swerving from the Mean, and correct, fitted to command reverence; accomplished, distinctive, concentrative, and searching, fitted to exercise discrimination.

All-embracing is he and vast, deep and active as a fountain, sending forth in their due season his virtues.

All-embracing and vast, he is like Heaven. Deep and active as a fountain, he is like the abyss. He is seen, and the people all reverence him; he speaks, and the people all believe him; he acts, and the people all are pleased with him.

Therefore his fame overspreads the Middle Kingdom, and extends to all barbarous tribes. Wherever ships and carriages reach; wherever the strength of man penetrates; wherever the heavens overshadow and the earth sustains; wherever the sun and moon shine; wherever frosts and dews fall—all who have blood and breath unfeignedly honor and love him. Hence it is said—"He is the equal of Heaven."

It is only the individual possessed of the most entire sincerity that can exist under Heaven, who can adjust the great invariable relations of mankind, establish the great fundamental virtues of humanity, and know the transforming and nurturing operations of Heaven and Earth—shall this individual have any being or anything beyond himself on which he depends?

Call him man in his ideal, how earnest is he! Call him an abyss, how deep is he! Call him Heaven, how vast is he!

Who can know him, but he who is indeed quick in apprehension, clear in discernment, of far-reaching intelligence, and all-embracing knowledge, possessing all Heavenly virtue?

It is said in the Book of Poetry, "Over her embroidered robe she puts a plain single garment," intimating a dislike to the display of the elegance of the former. Just so, it is the way of the superior man to prefer the concealment of his virtue, while it daily becomes more illustrious, and it is the way of the mean man to seek notoriety, while he daily goes more and more to ruin. It is characteristic of the superior man, appearing insipid, yet never to produce satiety; while showing a simple negligence, yet to have his accomplishments recognized; while seemingly plain, yet to be discriminating. He knows how what is distant lies in what is near. He knows where the wind proceeds from. He knows how what is minute becomes manifested. Such a one, we may be sure, will enter into virtue.

It is said in the Book of Poetry, "Although the fish sink and lie at the bottom, it is still quite clearly seen." Therefore the superior man examines his heart, that there may be nothing wrong there, and that he may have no cause for dissatisfaction with himself. That wherein the superior man cannot be equaled is simply this—his work which other men cannot see.

It is said in the Book of Poetry, "Looked at in your apartment, be there free from shame as being exposed to the light of Heaven." Therefore, the superior man, even when he is not moving, has a feeling of reverence, and while he speaks not, he has the feeling of truthfulness.

It is said in the Book of Poetry, "In silence is the offering presented, and the spirit approached to; there is not the slightest contention." Therefore the superior man does not use rewards, and the people are stimulated to virtue. He does not show anger, and the people are awed more than by hatchets and battle-axes.

It is said in the Book of Poetry, "What needs no display is virtue. All the princes imitate it." Therefore, the superior man being sincere and reverential, the whole world is conducted to a state of happy tranquility.

It is said in the Book of Poetry, "I regard with pleasure your brilliant virtue, making no great display of itself in sounds and appearances." The Master said, "Among the appliances to transform the people, sound and appearances are but trivial influences. It is said in another ode, 'His Virtue is light as a hair.' Still, a hair will admit of comparison as to its size. 'The doings of the supreme Heaven have neither sound nor smell.' That is perfect virtue."

THE GREAT LEARNING

WHAT THE great learning teaches, is to illustrate illustrious virtue; to renovate the people; and to rest in the highest excellence.

The point where to rest being known, the object of pursuit is then determined; and, that being determined, a calm unperturbedness may be attained to. To that calmness there will succeed a tranquil repose. In that repose there may be careful deliberation, and that deliberation will be followed by the attainment of the desired end.

Things have their root and their branches. Affairs have their end and their beginning. To know what is first and what is last will lead near to what is taught in the Great Learning.

The ancients who wished to illustrate illustrious virtue throughout the kingdom, first ordered well their own states. Wishing to order well their states, they first regulated their families. Wishing to regulate their families, they first cultivated their persons. Wishing to cultivate their persons, they first rectified their hearts. Wishing to rectify their hearts, they first sought to be sincere in their thoughts. Wishing to be sincere in their thoughts, they first extended to the utmost their knowledge. Such extension of knowledge lay in the investigation of things.

Things being investigated, knowledge became complete. Their knowledge being complete, their thoughts were sincere. Their thoughts being sincere, their hearts were then rectified. Their hearts being rectified, their persons were cultivated. Their persons being cultivated, their families were regulated. Their families being regulated, their states were rightly governed. Their states being rightly governed, the whole kingdom was made tranquil and happy.

From the Son of Heaven down to the mass of the people, all must consider the cultivation of the person the root of everything besides.

It cannot be, when the root is neglected, that what should spring from it will be well ordered. It never has been the case that what was of great importance has been slightly cared for, and, at the same time, that what was of slight importance has been greatly cared for.

IN THE Announcement to K'ang, it is said, "He was able to make his virtue illustrious."

In the Tai Chia, it is said, "He contemplated and studied the illustrious decrees of Heaven."

In the Canon of the emperor (Yao), it is said, "He was able to make illustrious his lofty virtue."

These passages all show how those sovereigns made themselves illustrious.

On the bathing tub of T'ang, the following words were engraved: "If you can one day renovate yourself, do so from day to day. Yea, let there be daily renovation."

In the Announcement to K'ang, it is said, "To stir up the new people."

In the Book of Poetry, it is said, "Although Chau was an ancient state the ordinance which lighted on it was new."

Therefore, the superior man in everything uses his utmost endeavors.

In the Book of Poetry, it is said, "The royal domain of a thousand li is where the people rest."

In the Book of Poetry, it is said, "The twittering yellow bird rests on a corner of the mound." The Master said, "When it rests, it knows where to rest. Is it possible that a man should not be equal to this bird?"

In the Book of Poetry, it is said, "Profound was King Wan. With how bright and unceasing a feeling of reverence did he regard his resting places!" As a sovereign, he rested in benevolence. As a minister, he rested in reverence. As a son, he rested in filial piety. As a father, he rested in kindness. In communication with his subjects, he rested in good faith.

In the Book of Poetry, it is said, "Look at that winding course of the Ch'i, with the green bamboos so luxuriant! Here is our elegant and accomplished prince! As we cut and then file; as we chisel and then grind: so has he cultivated himself. How grave is he and dignified! How majestic and distinguished! Our elegant and accomplished prince never can be forgotten." That expression—"As we cut and then file," the work of learning. "As we chisel and then grind," indicates that of self-culture. "How grave is he and dignified," indicates the feeling of cautious reverence. "How commanding and distinguished!" indicates an awe-inspiring deportment. "Our elegant and accomplished prince never can be forgotten," indicates how, when virtue is complete and excellence extreme, the people cannot forget them.

In the Book of Poetry, it is said, "Ah! the former kings are not forgotten." Future princes deem worthy what they deemed worthy, and love what they loved. The common people delight in what delighted them, and are benefited by their beneficial arrangements. It is on this account that the former kings, after they have quitted the world, are not forgotten.

The Master said, "In hearing litigations, I am like any other body. What is necessary is to cause the people to have no litigations." So, those who are devoid of principle find it impossible to carry out their speeches, and a great awe would be struck into men's minds—this is called knowing the root.

This is called knowing the root. This is called the perfecting of knowledge.

What is meant by "making the thoughts sincere," is the allowing of no self-deception, as when we hate a bad smell, and as when we love what is beautiful. This is called self-enjoyment. Therefore, the superior man must be watchful over himself when he is alone.

There is no evil to which the mean man, dwelling retired, will not proceed, but when he sees a superior man, he instantly tries to disguise himself, concealing his evil, and displaying what is good. The other beholds him, as if he saw his heart and reins—of what use is his disguise? This is an instance of the saying—"What truly is within will be manifested without." Therefore, the superior man must be watchful over himself when he is alone.

The disciple Tsang said, "What ten eyes behold, what ten hands point to, is to be regarded with reverence!"

Riches adorn a house, and virtue adorns the person. The mind is expanded, and the body is at ease. Therefore, the superior man must make his thoughts sincere.

What is meant by, "The cultivation of the person depends on rectifying the mind," may be thus illustrated—If a man be under the influence of passion he will be incorrect in his conduct. He will be the same, if he is under the influence of terror, or under the influence of fond regard, or under that of sorrow and distress.

When the mind is not present, we look and do not see; we hear and do not understand; we eat and do not know the taste of what we eat.

This is what is meant by saying that the cultivation of the person depends on the rectifying of the mind.

What is meant by, "The regulation of one's family depends on the cultivation of his person," is this—Men are partial where they feel affection and love; partial where they despise and dislike; partial where they stand in awe and reverence; partial where they feel sorrow and compassion; partial where they are arrogant and rude. Thus it is that there are few men in the world who love and at the same time know the bad qualities of the object of their love, or who hate and yet know the excellences of the object of their hatred.

Hence it is said, in the common adage, "A man does not know the wickedness of his son; he does not know the richness of his growing corn."

This is what is meant by saying that if the person be not cultivated, a man cannot regulate his family.

What is meant by, "In order rightly to govern the state, it is necessary first to regulate the family," is this—It is not possible for one to teach others, while he cannot teach his own family. Therefore, the ruler, without going beyond his family, completes the lessons for the state. There is filial piety—therewith the sovereign should be served. There is fraternal submission—therewith elders and superiors should be served. There is kindness—therewith the multitude should be treated.

In the Announcement to K'ang, it is said, "Act as if you were watching over an infant." If a mother is really anxious about it, though she may not hit exactly the wants of her infant, she will not be far from doing so. There never has been a girl who learned to bring up a child, that she might afterwards marry.

From the loving example of one family a whole state becomes loving, and from its courtesies the whole state becomes courteous while, from the ambition and perverseness of the One man, the whole state may be led to rebellious disorder—such is the nature of the influence. This verifies the saying, "Affairs may be ruined by a single sentence; a kingdom may be settled by its One man."

Yao and Shun led on the kingdom with benevolence and the people followed them. Chieh and Chau led on the kingdom with violence, and people followed them. The orders which these issued were contrary to the practices which they loved, and so the people did not follow them. On this account, the ruler must himself be possessed of the good qualities, and then he may require them in the people. He must not have the bad qualities in himself, and then he may require that they shall not be in the people. Never has there been a man, who, not having reference to his own character and wishes in dealing with others, was able effectually to instruct them.

Thus we see how the government of the state depends on the regulation of the family.

In the Book of Poetry, it is said, "That peach tree, so delicate and elegant! How luxuriant is its foliage! This girl is going to her husband's house. She will rightly order her household." Let the household be rightly ordered, and then the people of the state may be taught.

In the Book of Poetry, it is said, "They can discharge their duties to their elder brothers. They can discharge their duties to their younger brothers." Let the ruler discharge his duties to his elder and younger brothers, and then he may teach the people of the state.

In the Book of Poetry, it is said, "In his deportment there is nothing wrong; he rectifies all the people of the state." Yes; when the ruler, as a father, a son, and a brother, is a model, then the people imitate him.

This is what is meant by saying, "The government of his kingdom depends on his regulation of the family."

What is meant by, "The making the whole kingdom peaceful and happy depends on the government of his state," is this—When the sovereign behaves to his aged, as the aged should be behaved to, the people become final; when the sovereign behaves to his elders, as the elders should be behaved to, the people learn brotherly submission; when the sovereign treats compassionately the young and helpless, the people do the same. Thus the ruler has a principle with which, as with a measuring square, he may regulate his conduct.

What a man dislikes in his superiors, let him not display in the treatment of his inferiors; what he dislikes in inferiors, let him not display in the service of his superiors; what he hates in those who are before him, let him not therewith precede those who are behind him; what he hates in those who are behind him, let him not bestow on the left; what he hates to receive on the left, let him not bestow on the right—this is what is called, "The principle with which, as with a measuring square, to regulate one's conduct."

In the Book of Poetry, it is said, "How much to be rejoiced in are these princes, the parents of the people!" When a prince loves what the people love, and hates what the people hate, then is he what is called the parent of the people.

In the Book of Poetry, it is said, "Lofty is that southern hill, with its rugged masses of rocks! Greatly distinguished are you, O grand-teacher

Yin, the people all look up to you." Rulers of states may not neglect to be careful. If they deviate to a mean selfishness, they will be a disgrace in the kingdom.

In the Book of Poetry, it is said, "Before the sovereigns of the Yin dynasty had lost the hearts of the people, they could appear before God. Take warning from the house of Yin. The great decree is not easily preserved." This shows that, by gaining the people, the kingdom is gained, and, by losing the people, the kingdom is lost.

On this account, the ruler will first take pains about his own virtue. Possessing virtue will give him the people. Possessing the people will give the territory. Possessing the territory will give him its wealth. Possessing the wealth, he will have resources for expenditure.

Virtue is the root; wealth is the result.

If he make the root his secondary object, and the result his primary, he will only wrangle with his people, and teach them rapine.

Hence, the accumulation of wealth is the way to scatter the people; and the letting it be scattered among them is the way to collect the people.

And hence, the ruler's words going forth contrary to right, will come back to him in the same way, and wealth, gotten by improper ways, will take its departure by the same.

In the Announcement to K'ang, it is said, "The decree indeed may not always rest on us"; that is, goodness obtains the decree, and the want of goodness loses it.

In the Book of Ch'u, it is said, "The kingdom of Ch'u does not consider that to be valuable. It values, instead, its good men."

Duke Wan's uncle, Fan, said, "Our fugitive does not account that to be precious. What he considers precious is the affection due to his parent."

In the Declaration of the Duke of Ch'in, it is said, "Let me have but one minister, plain and sincere, not pretending to other abilities, but with a simple, upright, mind; and possessed of generosity, regarding the talents of others as though he himself possessed them, and, where he finds accomplished and perspicacious men, loving them in his heart more than his mouth expresses, and really showing himself able to bear them and employ them—such a minister will be able to preserve my sons and grandsons and black-haired people, and benefits likewise to the kingdom may well be looked for from him. But if it be his character, when he finds men of ability, to be jealous and hate them; and, when he finds accomplished and perspicacious men, to oppose them and not allow their advancement, showing himself really not able to bear them: such a minister will not be able to protect my sons and grandsons and people; and may he not also be pronounced dangerous to the state?"

It is only the truly virtuous man who can send away such a man and banish him, driving him out among the barbarous tribes around, determined not to dwell along with him in the Auddle Kingdom. This is in accordance with the saying, "It is only the truly virtuous man who can love or who can hate others."

To see men of worth and not be able to raise them to office; to raise them to office, but not to do so quickly—this is disrespectful. To see bad men and not be able to remove them; to remove them, but not to do so to a distance—this is weakness.

To love those whom men hate, and to hate those whom men love—this is to outrage the natural feeling of men. Calamities cannot fail to come down on him who does so.

Thus we see that the sovereign has a great course to pursue. He must show entire self-devotion and sincerity to attain it, and by pride and extravagance he will fail of it.

There is a great course also for the production of wealth. Let the producers be many and the consumers few. Let there be activity in the production, and economy in the expenditure. Then the wealth will always be sufficient.

The virtuous ruler, by means of his wealth, makes himself more distinguished. The vicious ruler accumulates wealth, at the expense of his life.

Never has there been a case of the sovereign loving benevolence, and the people not loving righteousness. Never has there been a case where the people have loved righteousness, and the affairs of the sovereign have not been carried to completion. And never has there been a case where the wealth in such a state, collected in the treasuries and arsenals, did not continue in the sovereign's possession.

The officer Mang Hsien said, "He who keeps horses and a carriage does not look after fowls and pigs. The family which keeps its stores of ice does not rear cattle or sheep. So, the house which possesses a hundred chariots should not keep a minister to look out for imposts that he may lay them on the people. Than to have such a minister, it were better for that house to have one who should rob it of its revenues." This is in accordance with the saying: "In a state, pecuniary gain is not to be considered to be prosperity, but its prosperity will be found in righteousness."

When he who presides over a state or a family makes his revenues his chief business, he must be under the influence of some small, mean man. He may consider this man to be good; but when such a person is employed in the administration of a state or family, calamities from Heaven, and injuries from men, will befall it together, and, though a good man may take his place, he will not be able to remedy the evil. This illustrates again the saying, "In a state, gain is not to be considered prosperity, but its prosperity will be found in righteousness."

THE ESSENTIAL SERIES

THE ESSENTIAL SERIES *by Golding Books*

∽

The Complete Confucius
The Analects, The Doctrine of the
Mean, and The Great Learning

The Essential Tales of Horror
Frankenstein, The Fall of the
House of Usher, Strange Case of
Dr Jekyll and Mr Hyde, The Picture
of Dorian Gray, and Dracula

The Essential Classic Romances
Pride and Prejudice, Jane Eyre,
Wuthering Heights, and The Age
of Innocence

The Essential Louisa May Alcott
Little Women,
Little Men, and
Jo's Boys

Shakespeare's Sonnets

The Essential L. M. Montgomery
Anne of Green Gables, Anne of
Avonlea, Anne of the Island, and
Anne's House of Dreams

Jean-Christophe Complete

The Essential Robert Louis Stevenson
Treasure Island, Strange Case of
Dr Jekyll and My Hyde, Kidnapped,
and The Master of Ballantrae

The Essential Classics for Leaders
Tao Te Ching, The Art of War,
Meditations, and The Prince

The Essential Tales of Wonder
Alice's Adventures in Wonderland,
Through the Looking-Glass,
The Wonderful Wizard of Oz,
and Peter Pan

The Essential Willa Cather
O Pioneers!, The Song of the
Lark, My Ántonia, and
One of Ours

The Essential Mark Twain
The Adventures of Tom Sawyer,
Adventures of Huckleberry Finn,
The Prince and the Pauper, and
A Connecticut Yankee in
King Arthur's Court

The Essential Jules Verne
Journey to the Center of the Earth,
From the Earth to the Moon,
Twenty Thousand Leagues Under
The Sea, and Around the World
in Eighty Days

& Frances Hodgson Burnett
The Secret Garden, Little Lord
Fauntleroy, A Little Princess,
and The Lost Prince

Books *by* NICHOLAS TAMBLYN

∽

*Noli Me Tángere by José Rizal: A Shortened
Version in Modern English with an
Introduction and Notes*

*Siddhartha by Hermann Hesse: Abridged and
Illustrated for Younger Readers*

Chill Vegan Cookbook (with Katherine Eglund)

—

96

THE GREAT BOOKS SERIES

∽

*Histories by Herodotus and The History of the
Peloponnesian War by Thucydides*

Aeneid by Virgil and Metamorphoses by Ovid

*The Pilgrim's Progress, The Life and Death of
Mr. Badman, and Grace Abounding to the
Chief of Sinners by John Bunyan*

*Oroonoko and Love-Letters Between a Nobleman
and His Sister by Aphra Behn*

Sense and Sensibility and Emma by Jane Austen

*The Scarlet Letter and The House of the Seven
Gables by Nathaniel Hawthorne*

*Twelve Years a Slave by Solomon Northup
and Thirty Years a Slave by Louis Hughes*

*Heart of Darkness and The Secret
Agent by Joseph Conrad*

*My Brilliant Career by Miles Franklin
and The Getting of Wisdom by
Henry Handel Richardson*

*A Room with a View and Howards End
by E. M. Forster*

*Dubliners and A Portrait of the Artist
as a Young Man by James Joyce*

and many more…

GB

CONFUCIUS lived from 551–479 BC. According to tradition, his ancestors had migrated from the Song state to the Lu state three generations before. A descendant of the Shang dynasty Kings through the Dukes of Song, his birthplace was in Zou, Lu state (near present-day Qufu, Shandong Province). In his early twenties, he is said to have worked in various government jobs, and as a bookkeeper and a caretaker of sheep and horses. When his mother died, as was tradition, he is said to have mourned for three years. He soon achieved fame and great reputation through his political and moral teachings. The principles he espoused largely reflected the values and traditions in China at the time. Rather than create a formal theory, Confucius desired that his disciples study, learning and mastering the classic older texts.

NICHOLAS TAMBLYN is an author of both fiction and nonfiction. He was formerly a journalist, public policymaker, filmmaker, and researcher with an animal rights organization. His time based in Bangkok and Manila has also influenced the subjects of his writing. He lives just outside Melbourne, Australia, with his wife, author and illustrator Katherine Eglund. For the latest posts and information, visit NicholasTamblyn.com and follow his updates on social media.

Printed in Great Britain
by Amazon